PRAISE FOR *LOSING* ...

"In articulating what is now gone, Mr. Cotter vibrantly evokes the sensations of life before the beginning of the end of his hearing [. . .]. Notwithstanding the personal catastrophe that deafness represents, it did give Mr. Cotter the ideal subject, transformed through literary grace, for a book. [. . .] *Losing Music* comes closer to expressing the transcendent sensation by nearly being music itself. Its author turned adversity into quiet triumph. Evidence that Mr. Cotter's ear is still keen for the melodies of language sings from every page." **—Wall Street Journal**

"*Losing Music* explodes an individual experience of illness into a cultural and medical reckoning; with a sociologist's rigor and a poet's lyricism, Cotter takes readers on an odyssey through the social history of disability, the brutal bureaucracy of the American healthcare system, and the intimate violence of living in a volatile body. But this memoir is just as much a love letter to sound itself as it is a chronicle of loss; your world will sound different after reading it." **—Oprah Daily**

"In his moving memoir, John Cotter anticipates a world without sound. *Losing Music* offers a compelling portrait of how deafness isolates people from even those closest to them. [. . .] More broadly, he also challenges us to better understand how any disability radically alters a person's sense of self."**—Washington Post**

"*Losing Music* is a stunning, expansively beautiful book. Not just because of John Cotter's precise and vivid language on a sentence level, but also because of how it moves so tenderly through the vanishing of sound, and not just sound, but songs—points of connection that can be taken for granted. And even beyond this reality, *Losing Music* is not solely a sad book. It is also a book of comforts, of joys, of closeness. I am thankful for all of its movements."
    —Hanif Abdurraqib, author of *A Little Devil in America*

"John Cotter brings sound to the page as something tactile: abrasive, elusive, fluid, textured, a current between body and mind. He fashions language into a velvety pocket in a harsh world. *Losing Music* is a phenomenal book about what it's like to be sick and suffering, and in it, I recognize not only the isolating nature of illness, but also a powerful intimacy with one's own changing self."

—Elissa Washuta, author of *White Magic*

"More than about Ménière's, *Losing Music* is a powerful addition to the memoir canon—hard-hitting, beautiful, profound—a story of finding safe ground in a world regularly buffeted by very rough seas." **—*The Millions***

"A vertiginous journey of loss and discovery triggered by the onset of an unpredictable and mysterious disability. With poetic energy, John Cotter describes the roaring and swirling particulars of Ménière's disease, while he grapples with universal questions of meaning and suffering. The memoir effortlessly blends personal stories with delightful deep dives into sound dynamics, inner-ear anatomy, and eighteenth-century author Jonathan Swift, who becomes a much needed friend—'articulate, accessible, free with his time,' and, I might add, darkly funny, dramatic, and brilliant, not unlike Cotter himself."

—M. Leona Godin, author of *There Plant Eyes*

"John Cotter's memoir contains some of the most elegant writing about music, diegetic sound, and the experience of hearing that I've ever read."**—Jasmine Dreame Wagner, *BOMB Magazine***

"Cotter's depiction of his struggles with his new reality and the absurdities of the American healthcare system offers deep generosity of heart, mind and spirit while avoiding easy clichés about illness and health. At once contemplative and propulsive, this book brings together everything I love about reading."

—Jennifer Wortman, *Westword*

"A fantastic memoir by a writer I've long admired. Smart, deeply moving, and spectacularly written. [. . .] Don't miss this one."
—Matt Bell, author of *Appleseed*

"This memoir helps us see and feel his own distinctive experience with deafness and vertigo but within that telling, Cotter also gives us new ways of understanding sound and music and human companionship and the will to live."
—Sarah Viren, author of *To Name the Bigger Lie*

"I think the hardest thing for a personal writer to do is think well and feel well at the same time. John Cotter's writing is bursting with as much intellect as heart. It's as clear eyed and incisive as it is moving. It's what nonfiction should be."
—Lucas Mann, author of *Captive Audience*

"A fascinating, heartbreaking, deeply personal story from one of the most talented essayists around. It's a book about art and illness, the betrayals of the body, and what is kept and what is lost as time goes by."   **—Justin Taylor, author of** *Flights*

"I'm not sure what I'd do if my body became a seemingly unsolvable mystery, and I can't know how I'd handle the fear, frustration, and despair, but I doubt I'd have either the fortitude or the imagination to do what John Cotter has achieved in this book. *Losing Music* is a remarkable memoir: unsettling, insightful, and gorgeously written. I'll be pressing this book into many people's hands."   **—Maggie Smith, author of** *You Could Make This Place Beautiful*

LOSING

MUSIC

ALSO BY JOHN COTTER

Under the Small Lights

LOSING
MUSIC

*A Memoir of Art,
Pain, and Transformation*

JOHN COTTER

MILKWEED EDITIONS

First paperback edition, published 2024 by Milkweed Editions
Printed in the United States of America
Cover design by Mary Austin Speaker
Author photo by Kirsten Rebekah Bethmann
24 25 26 27 28   5 4 3 2 1

Library of Congress Cataloging-in-Publication Data

978-1-63955-076-0

Names: Cotter, John, 1976- author.
Title: Losing music / John Cotter.
Description: First edition. | Minneapolis : Milkweed Editions, 2022. |
Includes bibliographical references. | Summary: "A devastating account
of the author's experience with the debilitating condition known as
Ménière's Disease that sheds urgent, bracingly honest light on both
the taboos surrounding disability and the limits of medical science"--
Provided by publisher.
Identifiers: LCCN 2022037597 (print) | LCCN 2022037598 (ebook) |
ISBN 9781571311948 (hardback) | ISBN 9781571317681 (ebook)
Subjects: LCSH: Cotter, John, 1976- | Ménière's disease--Patients--
Colorado--Biography. | Hearing disorders--Colorado.
Classification: LCC RF275 .C68 2023 (print) | LCC RF275 (ebook) |
DDC 617.8/82092 [B]--dc23/eng/20220830
LC record available at https://lccn.loc.gov/2022037597
LC ebook record available at https://lccn.loc.gov/2022037598

Milkweed Editions is committed to ecological stewardship. We strive to
align our book production practices with this principle, and to reduce the
impact of our operations in the environment. We are a member of the
Green Press Initiative, a nonprofit coalition of publishers, manufacturers,
and authors working to protect the world's endangered forests and
conserve natural resources. *Losing Music* was printed on acid-free 30%
postconsumer-waste paper by Versa Press.

for Elisa

Contents

II

LOSING
MUSIC

I

Illness and Paris are mutually exclusive terms;
Paris only likes healthy people, because it
only likes success, and illness is as much a
failure as poverty.

—*from* "LA MALADIE À PARIS"
by XAVIER AUBRYET, *trans.* JULIAN BARNES

Prelude

I was in the car the first time music seemed strange: the instruments less distinct, the vocals less crisp. I was driving a lot that year, two hours total on my commute to work and back up the northern New England coast. I kept needing to turn the volume higher, kept straining to make out the words, if there were words, or the melody. At first, this felt like an indictment of my memory: surely the bass was louder? Didn't the voices come in sooner? I blamed digitization, or my loud car. Something was missing.

Work was Marblehead and home was Boston. On my way south in the evenings I'd pull over at a public beach—or a private beach I could sneak onto—and I'd plunge into the water. Concrete debris cut borders on the sand. Rebar, reassurance of ruins.

Those forty minutes a day gave me an opportunity to clear my head, to let whatever thoughts needed to make it to me arrive safe. The rhythm of the water against the sand clarified my feelings in the way music could, gave feeling a pulse.

It was early September of 2008 when the ocean disappeared. The late summer sun found its horizon earlier each day, and the light was changing as I sloshed out of the water and started toward the parking lot, drying off with the pink towel a woman from Nahant had given me when I asked her where I could buy one. The breeze came from several directions at once—that time of year when the water is perfect and the air's a little cold.

But I couldn't hear the ocean. I couldn't hear bird calls or traffic. All I could hear was a roar inside my head, a noise so aggressive it seemed to blot out the sounds around me.

For months by then I'd been hearing a ringing noise off and on, an engine or a siren in my ears that rose unexpectedly and then disappeared. Doctors couldn't explain it, couldn't say how long it would last or whether it would continue to worsen. One minute I could hear as well as always and the next I'd have to lean too close to people, my ear nearly touching their mouths.

Everyone knows what happens to sound underwater: the full-head echo, slowed-down motors and shore voices. The sound I heard wasn't like that. It was made of several tones, high and low together, like a lawnmower near your ear and a plane not far away. It announced itself with clicks and whistles, changing the pressure in my ears, a kind of buzzy gravity, a planet made of static.

I turned back to find the ocean. And I saw it, a surface of uneven glass. And once I could see it again I felt as though I could hear it too. As I would learn in years to come, the brain remembers sounds surprisingly well—or convinces itself it does—and so when it wants to tell the story *I can hear*, it releases its chemicals to help itself mimic noises the damaged ears have lost. You can hear what's not there, and you can hear what was never there.

I worried the ground would start moving. It had been coming out from under me that last year in sudden vertigo attacks. They seemed connected to the noise, but they didn't invariably pair with it. I tried to ignore what was happening to me, climbing into my car and turning the music up high to overcome the roar.

Inconveniently, my preferred listening that summer tended to the lugubrious, to music that unfolded slowly with lots of dynamic shifts: all those great ECM recordings of simple and gut-stirring stuff, Gavin Bryars or the Hilliard Ensemble. Repeat the same musical phrase enough and it changes. The softness of the pieces brought me to attention, directed the traffic in my head.

Summer weekends I'd drive to Hartford to visit my old college friend Golaski. He'd sit me in his living room, pour me a drink, and walk me through the Led Zeppelin or Smashing Pumpkins that I'd tried and failed to connect with when it was popular, pointing out what had been new (and, so, important) and what I'd missed. After a few glasses I'd forget most of the details he was so painstaking with, but I loved hearing him talk about it, and I loved the sense that I was learning, bettering my understanding of these things that were so loved. Here we were listening to the MTV sound together, the one

I'd struggled to appreciate as a kid; I was learning the shibboleths late, at age thirty, carefully filing them away.

On my own, I preferred the blues, or pop that didn't stray far from the blues. Or jazz. Or instrumental stuff that was avant-garde in the 1980s and by 2008 felt full of what the future used to be: Laurie Anderson, Robert Ashley. For years I was notorious among my friends for abhorrent taste. It wasn't just young friends: sixty-year-olds hated what I played in the car every bit as much as twenty-year-olds did. We'd be driving along and laughing and I'd pop in Congolese rhumba icon Papa Wemba and everyone would be patient for a couple of beats. Then somebody would break in with "All right, what the hell is this?" and everyone else would second them. The CD would come out and some indie thing slid into its place.

What I loved about Papa Wemba singing "Awa Y'Okeyi," the piano version anyway, was the controlled, almost ritualistic swings of passion, the way the piano anticipated and then responded to his cries, and of course the fact that—as it was in Congolese dialect—maybe less than five million people on the planet understood the words (nobody not born in the Congo speaks all of the languages in which Papa Wemba sings, unless it's a handful of haggard Belgian contractors who can't seem to explain to the locals in French why they're stealing all the minerals. What was that about money? Well, if you want a whole dollar a day we're always looking for someone to dig through dirt . . .). Since the language is impenetrable, and any translation iffy, we're left with pure sound, and we can pour anything into it, any fear or catastrophe or yearning, any warning.

Even if our tastes begin as a pretense, they soon become who we really are, and one of the great lessons I'd learned was to periodically try to disrupt that ossification. I'd pick categories of sound and study them, heading off to the library with an empty knapsack and coming home with a dozen CDs of opera or early jazz or whatever was charting. I'd listen to all of them, save favorites, assemble secret playlists: a driving list, a jogging list, a list to send me to sleep.

As I ran along the north shore in 2008, I may have resembled a different version of my father. Dad was a jogger, too, back in the happy days when he was young and full of vigor. He'd run for miles though Mohegan Park and arrive home covered in sweat. He'd chase me though the house, frightening me a little, because he was a strong man and I was a child. Only a few years later he started drinking instead of jogging, then drinking through work, then drinking instead of work, then waking up at 3 a.m. to drink. Nights when he drank and lashed out he'd come into my room at midnight with two glasses of coconut rum. I was maybe fourteen by then. He'd hand me one and tell me the story of his life, always telling it the same way, always ending when he delivered his last briefing on the Cambodian cross-border operation to General Abrams and stepped onto the plane home at Tan Son Nhut. Sometimes he'd describe the last scene in *The Killing Fields*, how John Lennon's "Imagine" begins to play just as the Cambodian genocide-survivor Dith Pran—played by fellow genocide survivor Haing S. Ngor—tells his American colleague, a fellow journalist who'd abandoned him to the Khmer Rouge, "There's nothing to forgive."

"And that music picks up," Dad would tell me as I sipped the rum, "and he sings, *Imagine all the people, living life in peace.*" He never asked for forgiveness for the things he'd said and done while drunk; instead, he'd tell this story. And he'd head off to bed and I'd play the song on my portable CD player with my headphones.

In 2008 I was a hundred miles north of him, running across wet sand by the shore, smooth as beach glass. To make it harder on myself I'd move to the hotter and coarser and whiter sand uphill, the pebble grade with its seaweed hopping with tiny insects and sharp with shells, just past the reeds, the beach grass, and the arrogant weathered cabins at its edge.

I ran to keep my body sharp, and because I could already tell that body was failing. Not the usual slowing pace of the body aging, but something capricious, that weird noise that blotted voices at work and only confused people when I tried to explain.

I was editing medical newsletters in 2008. Each month I overdrew rent on my account and paid it back in the week that followed. I wandered a wealthy town at lunchtime and listened to NPR voices talking, almost casually, about an economic collapse. I'd had thirty years to make something of myself.

On the drive home I'd try listening to Tom Waits's "Town with No Cheer," a song about a real city, Serviceton, that sported a thriving bar and restaurant in the first half of the century, when passengers had to switch rail lines—and drank and ate while they were there—in order to continue their journey from Melbourne to Adelaide refreshed and at their ease. But with the advent of café cars and the joining of the rail lines the town dried up and disappeared.

What makes the song so moving for me is what I strained to hear on those drives, and in the end what I couldn't hear: the fade-in and fade-out of Waits's voice in the persona of a dry local. He begins every phrase with something like a shout and then winds down to a defeated whisper, like a drunk lamenting his sobriety. The harmonium and synthesizer sound, respectively, of carnival and defeat; they merge and blur.

When my hearing cut out, beginning in 2008 and increasing with time, songs like that one came to me as though from down the street, as though the speakers were shorting out, as though I didn't know the tune.

What I feared losing—the catastrophe that the roaring shadowed forth—wasn't just a series of structured sounds, but the world those sounds created, a world you could live inside: Bach on a snowy afternoon, hard blues on a long night's drive, the background mood in a restaurant or at a party (or, increasingly, any public space not yet colonized by ESPN on flatscreen TVs). Music is color. When you're young you're the hero of a movie, and the Heifetz you play in your car or the Velvet Underground you first try out sex to isn't just background, it's location and weather. You feel it on your skin.

So many of the big, meaningful scenes of my life have become centered, in my memory, around music, and not just concerts. I think of the time I spent every last dollar I owned on a three-disc set of *Einstein on the Beach* and put it into the stereo while I drank coffee and thought about finding a real job; from the first notes (the numbers, chanted) I felt like I'd walked into a new life. Or the time Golaski and I spent an hour driving through fogbound Portland, Maine, on a bargain book tour and playing Genesis's "Mama" over and over, not able to get enough of its brutal camp. There was the time Bill and I debated the respective merits of various Johnny Cash records on New Year's Eve as we apportioned drugs on the back of one of the jewel cases. Or when Jaime and I realized, after seven years, off and on, that it was finished between us, this time for good, but she hung around my tiny apartment all afternoon because neither of us wanted our new lives to start quite yet. I played her Samuel Barber's "Knoxville: Summer of 1915," and we listened to every note with perfect attention, her cigarette smoke uncurling above us.

Cigarettes, drugs: lots of music seems hopelessly bound up in *cool*. But obscure one-upmanship can be cruelly exclusionary. I remember eating dinner with a couple of friends in college when the conversation turned to indie bands and then to bootlegs and then to variants of those bootlegs and I was lost—were they scoring points against one another? Were they bonding? There were no smartphones then, so I took out a book.

But as much as I didn't care about new music then, by the time I ran along the Swampscott shore I was coming to regard stereos and overhead speakers as one of the major obstacles to human language. Just as I didn't understand how to share in the fruits of the cool in Bikini Kill and Run DMC when I was younger, now the sounds and rhythms that centered people around me, marked emotional turns, drove the economy, were becoming a kind of aural pain, obscuring the words I needed to understand.

I was worried about becoming no fun, transforming into the joykill who asks that the music—the background sound of good times, Shelley's "where the spirit drinks till the brain is wild"—be turned low or off. Part of the fun of the music at those parties, or in those restaurants and elevators and supermarkets, is the way it connects us with our past. You hear a bad Billy Joel song in the freezer aisle at Safeway and time is refuted: you're twelve years old, driving off to football camp, or to dancing class, your mother's station wagon one major metal antenna.

Back in college my friend Vita gave me an EP cassette she'd found in a free bin at Newbury Comics, from a local group called, I think, Fledgling, and while the A side didn't do much for me, the B side wouldn't let go. The name of the song didn't seem to appear on the tape, but the slow plucking of strings and the sudden rush of a woman's raw voice and the rhythm kicking in . . . well, I loved the song. And I carried that EP from apartment to apartment until I no longer owned a means of playing it. One bit of the lyrics always got to me, just as the tune moves to an upswing: "when there's so much out there you can't imagine / it's such a drag but it's so much better than me . . ." The way she held out that "so" both times, dug into the "better," clipped the "me" . . .

Twelve years later—maybe six months before my ears began to die—I was walking down Massachusetts Avenue in Cambridge, past the Lizard Lounge, and as I sometimes did on a whim when I had an hour to kill on a weekday night, I walked down to the grotto to hear whoever was playing.

Within a few minutes of my ordering a drink, I heard that deconstructed chord, and the same voice. Eileen Rose and the Holy Wreck was the band's name, and it was clearly her song, the same song Vita gave me in 1996. I didn't even know Vita anymore.

Sitting there, listening and longing, my heart fluttered into my throat. Every moment I'd lived with the song compacted, contracted. I felt absorbed and released and excited for hours after. In the days that followed I tried to explain to friends just how emotional it had been, but it's like trying to tell a dream.

A New Life

Elisa's alarm wakes me at 6:30 a.m. I'm not deaf all the time—I hear best in the mornings. I open my eyes.

Pinstripes of light. Fall asleep beside the same person for longer than a year, wake up beside them, and time seems to lock in place. Every morning in Boston is the same morning: oatmeal, fatigue, the drowsy chat, the short walk to the train. Then you live in Denver and suddenly time's forward motion becomes apparent in the change of light: a new intensity, pinstriping the room like it's burning the plaster.

I get out of bed and I listen. The roaring in my ears has grown so persistent and so loud in the last years that I've become credulous, ready to believe that anything might help because it's too hard to imagine nothing can. I've tried fad diets and meditation. Driving west with our belongings in the back of the car, I found myself hoping the change in elevation would prove beneficial—pop my ears back to health. Some days I wake up to the noise and

the pressure, and some days I wake up to the sounds of
Elisa breathing, the rustle of sheets.

Caffeine determinism: I drink a cup and fill my bag
with student papers the coffee graded last night. With my
coat and hat in place I walk back through the carpeted
bedroom, in boots, to kiss Elisa goodbye. We smile at
one another in the mornings. I heard perfectly when we
met six years ago. I heard less well only a couple of years
after that—those days when I ran along the beach—but
we smiled those mornings too. It's better than beginning
the day with words. Today we're lucky and I can hear her.

Aside from my ears, we've been lucky about a lot: her
Boston job agreed to let her work remotely from our new
home two thousand miles away, and I'm finally able to
teach all day. I'm hearing well enough this morning that
I can tell she's been hitting snooze for the last half hour.
Now she's switching off the alarm. I move for the door.

"Wait," she says, "are you having that meeting today?"

"Yeah, this afternoon. I'm a little terrified."

"She can't say no, right? Wouldn't that be illegal?"

I don't know. I should have researched disability
rights by now but I'm sick, not disabled: I can be cured.
Even if I knew them, disability rights might not help:
I'm a contractor; University of Colorado can fire me at
any time; they don't have to give a reason. But I kiss Elisa
and move for the door. I tell her I'll call if I can hear.

The plan for today is to teach at two different schools,
sixty-five miles of driving, conduct a difficult conversation with my boss, hold office hours at both schools, and
then return to Denver to rehearse the play I'm directing.

Out of all this, it's the classes and play I'll enjoy; the rest is dark intermission, time alone with the noise in my head.

Traffic is cloudy at 7 a.m. There isn't time to drive down Colfax, Denver's boulevard of broken dreams, though I like to see people walking in the morning. Colfax provides the best chance of that. After living in Boston for a dozen years, I physically miss the sense of proximate strangers, weaving past me as they charge toward invisible fates in the morning rush. Their grim faces lend me courage: we're in this together. Unlit taillights don't cast any warmth.

I'm adjuncting now, meaning I'm teaching college-level classes for two thousand dollars each, sometimes a little more, five classes at four schools. It won't make me rich but it's paradise at the edges. Where else could I be paid not only to learn about a different subject every day, but to discover subjects I'd barely touched: a week on captivity narratives at an art school in Lakewood, independent study on Korean short fiction for an international student, two weeks on GMO crimes at an engineering school, the Colorado School of Mines, my first stop this a.m.

One thing has got better about my ears since we arrived in Colorado—the vertigo hasn't happened. In Boston, in recent years, the roaring sound would appear of a sudden and rise and rise until the room spun, lurching walls that sickened and exhausted me. The world didn't stabilize for days, and I missed swaths of work. Elisa would sit beside me, reading aloud and stroking my hand. But such attacks seem to have cleared up since we came west. I've gone two years without one, and I don't want them to return and take over my life.

Vertigo to one side, even the ringing stopped when we arrived in Denver. For six months I luxuriated in quiet. I bragged on it to friends: "You know what I hear now? Just your voice. Watch: whisper something."

I also began to like Colorado. When I drove from the School of Mines to Lakewood, I'd change into shorts and boots in my car and hike up Green Mountain. It's a low mountain, hardly more than a hill, but bees hummed around mariposa lilies and I could feel my legs getting stronger and my breath coming easier the more often I forged up the slope.

I don't risk hiking while the ringing is back in my ear, but I play music when I can hear it. Lately it's been a reconstructed recording of an ancient measure, and I play it for some kind of reassurance that the past was real, that the world has persisted so long. It's a hymn, probably written in the fifth century BC. It's solemn plainsong and shimmering zither: unnerving and calming, both at once. As the song plays, I think about the Greek pantheon— overgrown teenagers with murderous caprices—and about the three Fates, who spin and spin the thread of your life and eventually snip it. Achilles knew when he was going to die but not how. Orestes killed under orders from a god, and the gods punished him for it.

The paradox of fate is that as much as it frustrates us, it consoles us too: "It could not have been otherwise." Fate exculpates us. As I drive I think back over my life and try to figure how I might have lived differently. If I'd known my ears would give out in my thirties, how would I have prepared? A life of pleasure would have left me uninsured. Padding my wallet would have required alternative talents. I couldn't have met Elisa when I was much younger—she was in Texas. How different a life would I have needed to live?

I'm clear of Denver by 7:35 and entering Golden. I can tell because the strip malls of Colfax disappear. A little "southwest" architecture has crept north this far: pine portals adorned with the stubs of corbels above their doors, like placeholders for future balconies. They're supposed to look unfinished like that: the stage set of the old west.

When I first heard of the Colorado School of Mines, I pictured a mineshaft leading to classrooms (the dark of the rock, the white of the notebooks), but it's beige brick and green sod. I park, cross campus, and arrive at my garden-level seminar room and begin to write on the board as the students file in behind me.

I write "Deontology, Virtue Ethics, Consequentialism": in short, Kant's golden rule, Aristotle's Good People Do Good Things, and Bentham's averaging-out.

Mines hires English teachers to run their ethics class

because it's also a composition class. In the course of teaching them how to write a college essay, I'm to introduce major ethical movements and pose a series of questions: What is the moral responsibility of an engineer? Does nature have intrinsic value or must it yield to all human desires, no matter how unbridled? Should we frack first and ask questions later?

Last Friday I tried to do this through almost total deafness and a sound like an oncoming Amtrak in both ears. Now I can hear a lot better. Voices rise as the room fills, or at least they do when I turn my right ear to the room instead of my left.

"We were talking about that old property on Monday," I say, "the old gas station your company's been hired to clean up. Your job is to test the ground contamination, and it's way too high here. Toxicity levels threaten a nearby water source. But your boss tells you to ignore it."

You're raised one way and then it's all over your face or all over your name. How much do we control what other people see in us? How much do we control the way we see ourselves?

"The honest thing is to go public with this information—people could be poisoned by this water—but it's going to set the project back and it might endanger your job. Charles, what does Aristotle think you should do?"

I want to get through this part quickly and Charles, ex-Navy, knows the answers. It's a cliché, but damn if military students aren't better prepared.

"Aristotle says you should behave virtuously," Charles reports, "and honesty is a virtue."

"Right, and interestingly loyalty isn't. But why would that be?"

Aristotle would approve of this style of teaching: dialogue. Out loud was how learning happened for the Greeks. As he wrote in his *Short Treatises on Nature*:

> It is hearing that contributes most to the growth of intelligence. For rational discourse is a cause of instruction in virtue of its being audible, which it is, not directly, but indirectly; since it is composed of words, and each word is a thought-symbol. Accordingly, of persons destitute from birth of either sense, the blind are more intelligent than the deaf and dumb.

The Greek word for deafness was *kophos*, dull or blunt.

I continue: "Whereas for Kant, what's the story? If we stay silent about the contamination, what are we saying with our silence?"

A crew-cut kid in the front puts his hand up. I feel guilty right away. He always tries to give me the answers but he's so soft-spoken I can rarely hear them. Today is different—I have a good strong left ear—and so I nod *go ahead*.

"Kant is the categorical imperative." He's right. And he knows it too, not a rare thing here at Mines.

"So by reporting the leak," I go on, "according to Kant everyone should report leaks all the time. And by *not* reporting it, we're making it a universal law that *nobody* should."

I hear a click when I swallow, like I'm changing altitudes. It's a symptom of the ringing ear getting worse. I know this but I try to tell myself otherwise.

"And utilitarians think what about the subject?"

Kophos: dull or blunt. Was that any less incriminating than the Oxford definitions of *dizzy* ("foolish or stupid") or *giddy* ("mad, insane")?

"Anybody—what do utilitarians think?"

The noise in my ear right ear hums louder now.

"Nobody remembers?" I'm still writing on the board. I take a long time to form letters, thanks to spelling trouble since I was a kid. It still comes up in stress. When I start to write a *W* on the board it keeps turning out a *Y*.

"Emma, you must know this: what would the utilitarians make of the gas station problem?"

I turn around to find Emma laughing. A few of the kids around the table are smiling along with her.

Her voice comes at me fainter than it should: "I've said the answer like four times now!"

"I'm a little *deaf* today, everyone!" I bug my eyes and exaggerate my voice. When I need their attention I act like a goof. "So today's a shouting day! Hurray, a shouting day!"

God bless Charles for nodding respectfully, like I'm his commanding officer. Some of the others look confused. I haven't told them much about the ear thing. I've just asked *what* a lot.

"I have a *whistle* in my right ear." I say this loud. "And until the doctors understand and can fix it, I need you guys to *face* me when you talk and enunciate big. Really use the diaphragm."

We go on like that for a while, but lots of them are shy and don't care for shouting. I've begun to suspect that some people physically *can't* shout. By now they can tell I'm struggling.

I'll switch gears. I'll involve them personally. So I ask a boy wearing sunglasses on my right what he would do under Kant's system of ethics, and I walk closer to him so I can catch his words.

"I wouldn't report it," he says. This is a more common answer than I'd expected, and I can't tell if the students who give it are serious. This particular boy is one I have an unhealthy prejudice against, perhaps because he looks exactly like a young Tom Clancy. I remind myself he's an engineering major; he understands how cross girders support cars on bridges and I do not.

"But then Kant's question is, what happens if people follow our example and nobody reports problems? Wouldn't dishonesty become endemic?"

Tom's talking but it sounds like muttering. The noise in my right ear is a teakettle now and I could swear just a moment ago the room jolted toward the left. Or am I imagining that?

"What was that?"

"You have to do what's best for your family," Tom says. "Like, your job is to protect your family. That's your job. So if you're doing your job well, you're protecting them. You gotta keep your boss happy."

I don't have enough money in the bank to quit my own jobs for any length of time, or to lose them.

"Protect your *family*?" I ask Tom. "But you're not married yet, are you? Do you have a bunch of kids we don't know about?"

The class laughs but Tom doesn't. Damn it—that was a dumb thing to say.

The noise in my right ear is a straight roar now, oscillating between the sound of a hair dryer on low and the sound of four hair dryers on high.

"The question is, what if *your* family drinks from that water source? Don't all families deserve clean water?"

Frustration spreads a red stain across my cheek.

The ancient Greeks tried to cure deafness with wool soaked in turpentine.

"Immanuel Kant says we all need to shout," I shout. "What were you whispering?"

There's little in ancient Greek literature about deafness. In Herodotus, King Croesus calls his deaf child "wretched."

"You're not going to get another job if you rat on your bosses," Tom says. "Keep the job you have."

Homer was blind but he was not deaf.

What is a sound but not a wave?

The tinnitus in my ear does not come from an outside stimulus. No one's sure where it comes from. The going theory has it the ear, when it dies, casts out signals in search of the noises it misses. Those signals are perceived as sound, hence the whistle, hiss, ratchet.

I've been visiting specialists of the ear for several years. It's striking how alike their diagnoses read: the ear is delicate, little is known, there are things we can name, but we don't understand enough to treat them. Eventually, every specialist reminds me of the last. They're stolid white men of upper-middle-class families, the sharp edges of temper smoothed by professionalism. I see them for about ten minutes each, and each of them shakes their head when I ask, "What's next?" Two use the same phrase: "Try to live your life."

I wish I could explain it better. If they understood how the roaring in my head assumed all the space inside and outside, pushing my thoughts out of reach, pushing the rest of the world into hiding, they'd want to break rules to help me. Even if it meant risking untested cures, catching up on new studies.

I try not to brood. I live my life, taking in the view from my car window on the commute between schools, the twice-weekly drive from the School of Mines to the University of Colorado. Highway 93 was built on manifest destiny: mineshafts covered in rotten boards, dark striations on the rock cuts like stains.

It's not the landscape I grew up with, but it's the landscape that hung on the walls of my boyhood home in New England. Dad loved the look of the west. I thought he'd feel a vicarious interest in my move here. Instead he was hurt, said he felt abandoned, predicted that I'd find only disappointment, that I'd screw up like I always did.

He was right that I was no stranger to mistakes. For a long time I'd had trouble understanding the rules of life, understanding other people. When I did achieve successes—winning a scholarship, or publishing a novel—Dad often phrased it in the language of con jobs. "You pulled one over on 'em, boy."

To grow up with an alcoholic—especially one as generally angry as Dad—is not unlike living a long time with a mysterious illness. It is to live at the mercy of a god with many faces, one who doles out rewards and punishments that don't seem commensurate with what's earned; because they're not commensurate, they're capricious. I tried to appease the god with superstition. I couldn't make things connect.

Thanks to whatever is happening inside my head—whether it's genetic or environmental or . . . what else could it be?—my own body has become that angry god, rewarding me with health or punishing me with sickness, with torture in the ears or with a few days of normalcy. I know this kind of living. I know how it pushes my own desires and moods to one side, how it dominates and overwhelms.

At least the world doesn't spin anymore, vertigo—the real destructor—in abeyance. I turn right onto Regent Drive. I'll finish this coffee, review my plans, lock the car. The small things, at least, I have in hand.

The kids in my 1:30 class at CU dress more expensively than the kids at Mines. One of the boys wears a suit—game day? Frat thing?

"Today we're going to do a quick exercise to get you all accustomed to looking closely at language. In groups, use Nancy Mairs's 'On Being a Cripple.' Okay, you four are a group; you four are a group; you, too, you got it. Et cetera! Go through it and look for at least four of the Greek rhetorical concepts we talked about. Look for metaphor, synecdoche, whole list. Find four." I raise four fingers.

So far, I haven't talked with any of the students here so much as talked *at* them. I'm typically friendlier—they like to razz me a little and vice versa—but this afternoon the few things I can hear arrive as if spoken through heavy fabric. It's not a warm room but I'm flushed.

"Just for example," I say, "the author of the piece pointing out a litotes here? She's not using one; she's pointing it out. She doesn't like 'differently abled,' she says, 'which partakes of the same semantic hopefulness that transformed countries from "undeveloped" to "underdeveloped," then to "less developed," and finally to "developing" nations.' So she's saying 'differently abled' is an ironic understatement, right?"

When I got the job here an older instructor pulled up a chair beside me at the coffee shop and said, "So what we encourage here is less top-down teaching. No more Sage on Stage, you know? No more pretending professors have the answers. I'm not a Sage on Stage, I'm a Guide on the Side. Put them in groups and let them teach each other—the kids know more than we do anyway."

I walk over to Kayla and Ashley's group to guide them from the side. I squat on my heels and find Kayla already talking to me. Fully aware of how it sounds, I tell Kayla I'll have to lean in to hear her. But Kayla doesn't make her words distinct enough either, so I ask her to repeat herself. She does, but speaks just as softly.

"Pro*ject*, Kayla." I catch myself. "It's my fault, not yours."

"We're looking for *litotes?*" she asks. I've got it this time.

So I explain the project again, worried I may be shouting to overcompensate. But something's different now. The noise in my right ear changes. Like the sound of an engine when a car shifts gears, the new noise is higher in pitch and twice as loud as that roar. It's amazing to me that Kayla doesn't hear it too.

"Look at the handout I gave you," I say to buy myself some time. The floor's moving. No—it's not. This happened at Mines too. But it's different this time. It really *does* seem to move.

All three kids are talking to one another now. My job is to listen in and help, but I can't hear what they're saying. I try again.

"Look, litotes is actually a bad example. Here, I can find one for you . . ." I remember where it is and turn Alex's pages.

I read the sentence aloud: "I miss picnics, dinner parties, poetry readings, the brief visits of old friends from out of town." I tell him that's an asyndeton—no "and" at the end. "Look for stuff like that, anything on the list."

"Troy," Kayla says, but not into my ear. "Natu . . . in . . . or I don't know."

Then I think I hear one of them say *hyperbole*. They are, they're talking about it. But everything Ashley says disappears. Something about something natural? I really am sweating now and I stand up, but standing up makes things seem like they're moving again. No.

I don't want to be here. I don't want to talk about an essay about being a cripple because I'm not a cripple—I'm just sick and we'll fix it. We'll fix it and this will be a little lost time and I'll make it up. Nancy Mairs seems like a tough dame but I'm not like her. I'll be cured.

There's a glass sculpture in Barbara's office but I can't focus enough attention to remember for more than a second what it is. An apple? Pencil tray? I concentrate only on Barbara's face, trying to hear the shapes of her words. This is going to be a difficult conversation and it's starting right now. She's asking me what I came in for.

"Something is happening to my ears," I say. I smile in a way I hope she finds disarming. "It sounds stupid but I promise you it's true. My hearing is cutting out. It cuts out and comes back and cuts out. It's happened in the past but it's worse now." I know how crazy that sounds. I also know I must look pale and scared.

No expression crosses her face. Of course she has to be cautious not to seem too sympathetic, not to come straight out with *that sounds difficult,* or *what do you need to do the job,* or anything that leaves an open question. I talk about it for a few sentences more but her face remains cool. She has to function as an official, and I have to be the one who bends. Okay, this makes sense. This is adjuncting.

She expects me to keep talking. I've told her the problem and now she wants to hear the solution I have prepared. "I looked into a program that provides hearing aids to teachers in Colorado, but the federal sequester froze their budget. So I'm just going to buy them. But I may need over a week off before they come in. It might be two weeks."

Two weeks.

The glass sculpture on her desk goes blurry for a half a second. Nerves.

She says, "I see." She says it as carefully as I listen. Her voice is strong and we sit close in the quiet room.

"Our preference"—here's where it happens—"In this kind of situation, we would ask that you resign."

It's April. If I resign there'll be no more work until early June at another school, and then only if I'm healthy enough. I'll be short of money two months, and with hearing aids to buy. You can't find college jobs midsemester. There are fewer classes open in summer months.

"Is there another option?"

"If you want to fulfill your contract," she says, her expression as blank as I've ever seen, "you'll need to find a substitute, we'll need to approve them, and you'll need to pay them from your own pocket. There's a chance I may be able to help you with some names . . ."

She helps me with some names. As she talks, I subtract numbers in my head. Food and gas. Rent and doctors. Time lost.

· · ·

April snow. "You always know when it's going to snow in Boulder," a local friend had told me, "because it smells like cowshit first." Greeley, in the north, has cows.

Stepping out of Barbara's office, I orient myself in the still-unfamiliar landscape by finding the oldest building. There, the one with the mansard roof and gothic arches. Based on the look of it, the builders are long dead. They probably did their work about a hundred years before I was born. The mountains behind that roof are obscured by clouds, but I can feel them through the air because it's thin. Soon it will be dark. I'm a stranger in someone else's house.

But my ears aren't ringing. For a long time, I've wondered if stress makes the noises worse. This little relief seems to belie that fear. I can hear the silence in the quad, or something close to it. There's a faint barrel roll at the back of my right ear, but it's hardly there. It's the kind of thing you can tune out. I hope there's enough background noise in my office to tune it out.

CU mandates office hours. Once they run out of room in the rhetoric department, adjuncts wind up in an upper floor of the CU stadium, about half a mile from where I teach. As I walk there through the flakes and the lights, I can make out clear sounds of traffic, crunching boots. I hear my own breath. Snow doesn't make a sound as it falls. It isn't cold.

Despite what happened in Barbara's basement office, I feel relieved. No, I don't know how I'll pay someone to take my place, or where I'll find the money for hearing aids. But maybe it's over, all of it. Maybe this silence means the roaring stays gone.

I hear my own footfalls through the stadium's concession stands, echoing off the grills down over the booths. Through a hidden door, up an elevator, and down two connecting halls, I arrive at my office. The floor where it's situated feels abandoned for the night. Since I didn't know whether I'd be at CU any longer than a semester, I haven't stocked the place with personal things. I start up the PC on my desk and go straight to social media. I'm craving the simulation of community there—the sense of people talking in a way I can hear with my eyes. The sense that my friends will be there when I'm healthy and I return.

One of my Mines students, Duncan, has sent me a friend request that I'll have to decline—I don't friend current students—but I click his profile anyway. Here's what I see: blond Coloradans in rows, all of them in the same sweatshirts, each of them paler than newborn ewes, and each one of them set up with Duncan's own chin, nose, and ears. The girls are long-haired Duncans. The elders are Duncans with jowls.

I'm thinking of fate again as I leaf through the images. My own family is small: four blood relatives, new nephew included. But the family resemblance has spread to my nephew, and he wears the same sleepy eyes I had when I was a kid, and still have. I hope he'll live a healthy life. But that isn't all up to him. I close Duncan's page and scroll through my Facebook feed: fellow teachers solicit exercises from the hive. Clips of songs. Sponsored ads for local auto parts. New babies. Nostalgia.

A new sound. My left ear, quiet all evening, clicks and whistles on: the sound of a teakettle two rooms away. In the glow, in the dark room, I feel it coming obscurely, a queasiness in my stomach, a sense of something I can only call *unreality*. I have just enough time to lie down on the floor, pull the metal trash can next to me in case I vomit, and punch Elisa's number into my phone to tell her I won't be able to drive myself home tonight.

Like a spring released, the room rocks away from me. It's like drinking so much you can't tell up from down, except that I'm sober and sleep won't fix it. I'm stuck here now, watching the room twist, sick from it.

As the last light disappears outside, I sit in the dark and despair of the feeling in my nerves, the anxiousness of falling, the involuntary grasping of my hands on the carpet. The lines around things go wavy, swing left, left, invisibly resetting and swinging left. Then it picks up speed.

"I'm having a vertigo attack," I say to Elisa when she answers the phone. It's been two years.

"Oh, shit," she says. "Oh, I'm sorry. Can you hear enough to talk?" Two things are true: I need a ride home and I have our only car. "Shit. Okay. Okay, I think Aaron's in Boulder. Can you hear? I'll call him."

"Two *fuck*ing years."

Elisa calls back a few minutes later with a plan: our friend Aaron will take the bus to campus, then drive me, in my own car, to Denver. If need be, he'll walk to the stadium first and collect my keys, so he can fetch the car and drive it closer. The only catch is the fire door to the hall: it's locked from the outside. In the next ninety minutes, I'll need to get myself out there.

It gives me something to think about apart from my own misery. Good, okay. I rise to all fours and begin to move down the hall, rocking my hips and shoulders into the wall every few feet. Because of the sort of vertigo I experience, I alternately feel as though I'm crawling on the floor, wall, ceiling. That's less fun than it sounds: my reptile brain is constantly alarmed. I don't want to feel scared; my prefrontal lobe knows I'm on the floor and that I can't fall far. But the rest of my brain is in charge of the full-body signals too, and its reflexes want my back on the ground, want the ground to stay the ground.

I do reach the door and prop it open with a shoe. By the time Aaron arrives, the vertigo's abating, my heart rate is normal again, but I know from experience that I won't be good on my feet for days. Vertigo attacks come in clusters, and between them the world doesn't quite settle down. Two days later, I'll feel the way most people feel when they describe themselves as "a little dizzy," and I'll be grateful.

Sound Shadow

I needed hearing aids, and because I needed them, I didn't want them.

"According to this chart your loss is considered moderate."

"But it goes away," I said, convinced this expert wouldn't believe me. "Sometimes I can hear just fine."

"Okay, yes, I'm seeing that here too. Wow, you test all over the chart."

Melinda was the first audiologist I'd spoken to in my thirty-five years on Earth, and she trusted I was telling her the truth. Physicians weren't like that. But audiologists are either PhDs or AuDs, not MDs: they study not only the ear but the dynamics of sound. After World War II, the large number of GIs coming home with bomb-wrecked ears created the need for a profession trained in taking care of them: audiology. Unlike physicians, whose job is to diagnose you, audiologists are required to be creative, to give you room to explain.

I liked Melinda, but I'd been tricked into meeting her.
"I think I *do* have something that can help you," a physician had told me, after ten minutes of pleading on my
part, pleading and bitching. With a glint in his eye, he
packaged me off to Melinda's examination room without
explaining who she was or why we were talking. To my
alarm, Melinda wasn't a diagnostician after all. An audiologist was someone who prescribed machines you had
to buy. They didn't cure you, just made things louder.

"You can choose from in-the-ear and behind-the-
ear models. Behind-the-ears are going to offer more
options."

"What would that cost me?"

She paused.

"There's a variety of price ranges. So there are options. For someone with fluctuating loss like yours the
more expensive models, again—I'm thinking about a
six-thousand-dollar pair from Widex that might be able
to offer more flexibility and, given the nature of your
loss, might wind up being the best fit for you."

"Are they covered by insurance?"

"They're not, I'm sorry."

By then I'd been to doctors in LA and Boston and
Denver and none of them had good news. Here in this
room with Melinda, I opened my mouth to object to any
testing, any fitting, but I found, to my surprise, that I
lacked the will. So she rose and I rose, and I let her lead
me away to the sound-treated room.

. . .

Gray walls and a bolted-down chair center stage, draped with audio cords. The sound treating removed any voices or footfalls or equipment humming from wires or pipes, leaving me nothing to listen to but the roar in my head. I nearly said, "It's loud in here."

"Let me know if this is uncomfortable." Melinda pushed flexible earphones into my ears, placing them in far enough they'd avoid any errors from diffraction—no sound hitting obstacles on its way to me and changing as it bent around them. Sound passes *through* some obstacles, of course, but those sounds can weaken and change as a result. When such obstacles become so intrusive as to obscure the sound completely, they're known as sound shadows: a wall too thick to hear behind, a wind to take your words away. A physical shadow seemed like a good metaphor for whatever was going on inside my ears: sound was darker on this side of it, the warmth of human noises muted or void.

Melinda disappeared from the room and into the adjacent booth. There was a window between the booths, but my chair was turned away from it. If I couldn't see her face when she spoke into the microphone, I'd find it harder to know what she said, and in fact that was the point. According to Dr. Jess Dancer, a professor of audiology quoted in Katherine Bouton's *Shouting Won't Help: Why I—and 50 Million Other Americans—Can't Hear You*, "It's not unusual for speech intelligibility to increase from 20 percent when listening in noise without vision, to 80 percent or more when the speaker is seen as well as heard." We hear with all our senses at once.

"Can you hear me now?"

"Yes but you're way too loud."

"How about now?"

I tried to distract myself by picturing the sound-starved neurons misfiring in my ears, creating the feedback signals I misread as noise. As I tried to imagine the auditory centers of my own brain, the neural networks of fibers far thinner than spider's silk, constellations and ligatures pulsing off and on all night and day, I thought too of the shapes sounds make in the air, the way we come up against them.

Air molecules are always moving, colliding and wandering back, but we can lend them direction by widening and narrowing the vocal folds in our throats as we force more air out of our chests. At the speed of sound, 343 meters per second, those molecules we've agitated strike the eardrums of our listeners. In turn, those eardrums agitate the three small bones of the ear, which clack out patterns on the cochlea, the coiled snail in its bony chamber, where the force of the sound converts to electrical signals, carried straight to our brain on cranial nerves; their destinations are the specialized regions of our temporal lobes that relate electrical patterns to sounds we've heard in the past.

Along with auditory centers, visual and language centers too can be found in the temporal lobe, just above your ears, straight behind your eyes. It's a region of the brain that's especially important to memory, particularly long-term memory. The ability to translate noises into linguistic meaning is inextricable from how the hearing see the world, and how we hold on to what we've seen and heard.

As I listened to the noise in my own head, I felt something nudging those very neurons. Or did I? It came from my ear, through the wires snaking back to the audiometer. I wasn't sure, but I thought it was a tone. Or just the intimation of a tone: a hum I couldn't pin. Then it became clearer. A high sound. I thumbed the button. Melinda saw I'd responded and selected the next frequency in the test. I clicked. Then the next.

Sounds are pressure waves: when they appear closer together, that means we'll hear a given tone as a high one: trumpets and piccolos. When the pressure waves move farther apart, the tones drop lower: cellos down to kick drums. Melinda was an old hand at this kind of work, alternating the sounds to create a map, one that showed her exactly what my ears could perceive and what they missed. I found myself anxious to catch even faint sounds. Sometimes I clicked at what could only have been ghosts.

I wanted to pass this test, leave the office without permanent electronics of my own. But there were long stretches of what felt to me like silence. Except that it wasn't silence. It was a series of waves that, if you drew them, might resemble the ocean on a nearly still day: low, infrequent ripples. I just didn't know they were there.

. . .

This wasn't my first encounter with a mystery illness. At fourteen years old, I started experiencing strange aches at the back of my head. Shouting, exercising, bending over, the back of my head grew loud with pain that compelled me to lie down right away—on as flat a surface as I could find, typically the floor—until it ebbed. I wanted to join a dance troupe at school, but the headaches ruled out an audition. I rehearsed a short play for acting class entirely on my back. ("This is awkward," said one of the girls I directed from the pavement. "Don't look at *me*," her friend answered, "you're the one who *likes* him.") With my parents, I watched a George Carlin special on TV, but when I laughed, I winced. One joke—I don't remember which—got me laughing so hard I couldn't stop. I didn't watch him from then on, I just listened from the floor as I laughed through the pain.

Doctors couldn't make sense of it. Our local internist thought it was a symptom of anxiety. I *was* anxious, but the headaches were why I was anxious. I'd grown fast—were they "growing pains"? For a while, we settled on "migraines," and so it was migraines I pleaded when I needed to lie down on the floor of a classroom, or when I begged off going swimming at the beach. I still sometimes use the word today when I'm having a vertigo attack, partly because the illness may well be related to the migraine impulse, and partly because it's the word in the English language that best explains the sort of solitude I'll need to endure the attack—it's a word that says, "Fuck off, I'm in pain."

I thought of those headaches in Melinda's chair because I'd caught myself reciting some Shakespeare in my head. Those headaches were what started me on the habit. I was a theater kid, and that's what led me to discover I could do something most of the kids around me couldn't: I could remember Shakespeare. After a few runs through, swaths of text would get stuck in my head and I could recite them back anytime I was asked. I was not asked often; those kinds of parties don't exist. But I didn't have many remarkable talents as a kid, and so I clung to this one. It made me seem smarter than I was.

At fourteen, in thrall to the headaches, I'd practice on the floor to dampen the pain. I'd gotten ahold of my mother's college copy of *Richard II*, and I read the glue apart. My favorite passage came after Richard's rival usurped his kingdom and imprisoned him in the tower. From his cell, at least in Shakespeare's version of events, Richard delivers one of the strangest poems I'd heard. He begins, "I have been studying how I may compare this prison where I live unto the world." There's not much similarity between the prison cell and that world, and so he invents mental creatures to people it, little brain-children he sets through the motions. In the midst of all this, he's interrupted by music. He probably imagines the sound, but a good director will make it appear:

Ha, ha! keep time: how sour sweet music is,
When time is broke and no proportion kept!
So is it in the music of men's lives.
And here have I the daintiness of ear

To cheque time broke in a disorder'd string;
But for the concord of my state and time
Had not an ear to hear my true time broke.

I thought about this passage all the time when my
hearing started going. I ran through the sounds of it as a
way of hearing words when words disappeared. I couldn't
hear them spoken aloud on bad days, but they were perfect in my imagination; they were pure.

Pure tones—not metaphorically pure, actually pure—is
the proper term for the sounds Melinda sent through
my head. A pure tone is a tone that plays at one frequency
at a time, one set level of volume kept steady for each.
Real sounds out in the world aren't pure, metaphorically
or otherwise. Life noises—wind, cars, doors, rustling
fabric—exist as complex waves of any number of frequencies at once, both loud and soft sounds emerging in
a single breath. When you speak words such as "fix" or
"shut," they surface with a hiss of air, grow louder and
more resonant, close with a click and a whisper, proceeding as a single, constantly changing string of frequencies,
each phoneme a collection of measurably distinct pressure patterns, striking a listener's ear with varying force.
It turns out there's no such thing as a pure word.

But tuning forks can make pure tones. So can syn-
thesizers. Audiologists have equipment to make them
too, and that's what Melinda sent through my ears from

the booth: lone waves of pressurized air. There were no obstacles, no sound shadows, for the waves to diffract against, no interfering noise, no change in the velocity of sound from earphone to eardrum. I clicked the button in my hand to indicate the sounds I heard, and I clicked again for phantom sounds. I didn't know which sounds were real.

The news arrived as expected: I heard most of the sounds she played, but only just. I heard high sounds better than low ones. If this was progressive, I would probably lose them all. Meanwhile, at least in my case, sound would come and go.

This put me at a disadvantage among those who come to deafness late. Most late-deafened people suffer presbycusis, an age-related loss of hearing. In presbycusis, the hair cells in the inner ear start to die from the outside in. This could happen to me too, of course—it happens to most people if they live long enough—but that wasn't my trouble now. People with age-related hearing loss lose high sounds and I was losing low ones. My ear was dying from the inside out.

She gave me a lanyard to wear around my neck, like a medal of ill fortune, that could double as a microphone—the hearing aids had microphones too, but the lanyard could talk to my phone, so long as I held the phone close to it and pressed the right buttons . . .

I'm white, male, cisgender—for someone in a position of such social privilege to find himself falling into any amount of marginalization is a shock. I grew up during a period of increasing recognition of disabled people:

the Americans with Disabilities Act was signed into law during my childhood. American Sign Language was becoming a common mode of teaching Deaf students throughout the 1980s and early '90s. I'd have been badly disappointed in myself if I looked down on disabled friends.

I felt ashamed to feel ashamed.

What I wanted, after all, wasn't an expensive device but a total cure. Like the kind I'd been lucky enough to find at age fifteen, after visits to neurologists and tests and electrodes and the check-in procedures for the pediatric unit at Yale New Haven Hospital. I was a few months too young for the adult unit's sixteen-year cutoff, miffed but easily mollified: there were free cups of Jell-O in the game room's minifridge and you could draw whatever you liked on your own room's wall. I wrote out scenes from Shakespeare on the whiteboard across from my bed. Through with *Richard II* by now, I'd moved on to my grandfather's hardcover *Collected*.

It was a Yale neurosurgeon who'd diagnosed the cause of the headaches, a rare condition called Arnold-Chiari malformation. Back when I was a fetus, somehow, a portion of brain tissue formed itself in the wrong direction, angled downward into my spinal canal. It didn't start causing pain until my body changed, growing a foot taller in the course of seven months. Now I had to get it corrected or it might progress, might even paralyze me.

It was already hard to live with—the pain shot up when I coughed or sneezed. The treatment involved chipping away some vertebra and skull—less than an ounce, if all went well—and letting them stay chipped, giving the brain room to settle. Total nine hours on the operating table and a few weeks in bed while my spinal fluid replenished its stores.

They wheeled me to the room, showed me the Jell-O and the whiteboard, and asked me if I'd be able to fall asleep. I said I was wide awake and so they gave me sleeping pills, but the pills only made me high. At about 2 a.m. I put aside my book, opened a magic marker, walked over to that blank white wall and copied out the Duke's prison monologue from *Measure for Measure* in blue ink ("Thou hast nor youth nor age, / But, as it were, an after-dinner's sleep, / Dreaming on both").

Waking up a few days later, I found fifteen-year-old Jeff at the foot of my bed with a chessboard, the Duke's monologue half-erased behind him. The words were green.

"I thought I could teach you to play and then we could play a few games. Now, first, with your permission, I'm going to show you a trick to win in three moves every time, so long as your opponent doesn't know the trick first."

When I started falling ill in my thirties, Jeff suggested the cause might be that childhood sickness we'd played chess through in the common room at Yale New Haven Hospital, me spooning Jell-O into my dry mouth as he explained why my earliest moves on the board might be misguided ("I'll give you a chance to

take that back—then you can take it or choose not to—
but first let me show you why you might").

Once I was dizzy enough to need a cane most of the
time, Elisa drove me to a couple of specialists to investigate the Chiari connection. I even called the surgeon
who fixed me up at age fifteen. As far as he could see
there was no connection at all—the MRIs showed I'd
healed okay; case closed. I told one specialist that I still
felt suspicious about those old headaches and this strange
new disease. I pled my case: "The same things that make
my hearing worse now—standing up really quick, exercise, yawning—used to make my head hurt as a kid."

She asked me to stand up and sit down a few times
quickly, then asked her assistant to get her a blood pressure cuff.

"That's what I thought," she said as she took the cuff
off my arm, "you exhibit hypotension. It's probably because you're deconditioned."

"Well of course I'm deconditioned *now*—I can hardly
walk—but when I was jogging every day, standing up
quickly made the ears ring worse."

She shrugged. "It might just be because you're tall."

"I'm convinced this is fixable," a now-grown Jeff told
me on the phone, on one of the mornings I could hear
well enough to use it. "There's something obstructing
your hearing, and if you could take that thing away
you'd hear again."

Jeff fundraised cash for women's health nonprofits by then, working from an office of his own, with some time to kill between projects here and there. He killed it by putting up with my fretting.

"What especially worries me," he said, "is communication between you and Elisa. If you become unable to communicate, that will be bad."

"But Jeff, *that's* why we're seeing all these doctors. Jesus, man, the sooner we can get this cured, the sooner everything starts to get normal again."

He changed tack—or did he? "You remember Shanna?" A poet we'd known in New York. "She has hearing aids and she can get police radio on hers. She can turn people's volume up and down in her pocket. It's like superpower ears. It makes *me* want them."

And it was true that something had to change. By then, most mornings, I couldn't hear well enough to use the phone. The new devices promised to fix that.

Outside Melinda's office, I called Elisa on the lanyard they'd given me, one designed to pair up with the aids thorough a magnetic coil and transmit the signal directly from my phone.

When I heard her voice answer—or *a* voice—it sounded unrecognizable. I caught the electronic squeaks of words, muffled and robotic.

"Hang on," I said, fussing with the volume. "Hang on, maybe it's where I'm standing. Can I call you back to try again?"

I was nearly at my car by then, so I walked back toward the hospital. I'd had a signal there when I called

Elisa on the way in. "Hey, I'm trying again. Is this any better? Say a line or two more so I can tell if I hear you. Okay. Okay, this isn't working. I'm going to hang up. I'm sorry, I just can't hear you. I'm going to go."

It's no coincidence that being fitted with mechanical devices coincided with the sharpest pricks of shame I'd felt since the sickness began. Shame, after all, is built into the way such devices evolved: toward camouflage, deniability. The feeling their wearers too often experience is what Peter N. Stearns, in his book *Shame: A Brief History*, calls "one of the oldest traditions of group shaming: the sense that the disabled were shameful in themselves and that their existence brought shame to the families that bore them." The pack leaves its lame in the lurch.

Electronics were only the latest solution I'd tried. Before it occurred to anyone to fit me with hearing aids, I was in the habit of cupping my hand to my ear to increase the loudness of sounds around me. This is a good, if basic, technique: it can raise environmental sound by six decibels, or enough to lift a conversation from the background to the foreground, or to transform a whisper into speech. But it doesn't inspire self-regard. And over time it grew less effective: the deafer you are, to a point, the louder the world needs to be. If you want to lift the sound of a waterfall by twenty or thirty decibels—transform it from the far-off sound of a babbling creek into something monstrous—you can't rely on your hand alone.

We're familiar with ear trumpets from old-time pictures and cartoons. The daft uncle who still can't hear even *with* one ("What's that, sonny?"). Most scholars trace these back to the seventeenth century, but it would be haughty to assume our ancestors couldn't have rolled leaves into cones, or hollowed out auroch horns, or gone looking on a nearby beach for shells.

Among the acoustical artifacts of which we're certain, the oldest was made a bit over three hundred years ago. It's two feet of blown glass with a flare at the end—a sparkling coronet, hardly concealable or subtle. This wouldn't do. Swiftly, makers emerged, some of them, like Frederick Rein, exploring a new commercial market, rich with fattened bourgeoisie desirous of staying in the game. Rein made his ear trumpets of brass and painted nearly all of them black—the easier to blend into pre-electric murk. The richer you were, the more concealable they could be made. The poor, like now, made do with what they could. They made do with cupped hands.

Take the case of King John VI of Portugal, for whom Rein devised an "acoustical chair." When the regent toured his empire, subjects were instructed to kneel before the armrests, hammered into shape of lions' maws. Unbeknownst to those subjects, their voices poured straight down the lions' throats to a hidden resonating chamber, only to emerge—far louder—from a tube by the emperor's ears.

By the middle of the nineteenth century, so-called speaking trumpets and speaking tubes achieved mass-market potential. As did quackery. Handheld fans to relieve the heat ("Goodness, this stifling air! And now what was that, again?") could be fitted with openings and resonators. Nod and smile along at a concert and, every once in a while, discreetly touch the handle of the fan to your teeth. Bone conduction does the work and, according to the fan's marketing materials, "Music is heard perfectly with it when without it not a note could be distinguished."

Hearing devices were snuck into compacts for women and beige-colored pocket cases for men. By the middle of the nineteenth century you could get two earphone horns connected by a headband, and by the beginning of the twentieth century those horns had moved to the top of the head and might be concealed within a handsome wig.

Shame was a powerful tool for the Victorians—as it remains for us today—and if taboos against disability couldn't be enforced privately, they'd be enforced publicly. In America, these strictures took the form of a series of "Ugly Laws." From the 1860s to the 1970s, many of America's major cities mandated the removal of poor, diseased, and visibly crippled bodies from the public eye. It's no coincidence those laws began in the years that followed the Civil War—when the numbers of wounded and crippled rose dramatically—and only came to a close with the liberation movements of the early 1970s.

Susan M. Schweik, in her comprehensive study of the subject, *Ugly Laws: Disability in Public*, points the reader to the decision in Haller (1877), where "a New York appeals court ruled that disabled bodies in and of themselves could in fact constitute a form of speech—begging speech—and that the exercise of this kind of speech was punishable."

In such an environment, it wouldn't do to be spotted in public with a foot-long ear horn, or to stand in wind gusty enough to uncover the acoustical tubing beneath your wig. The disabled only became a protected class within my lifetime, and within that lifetime I've watched my elected representatives vote to roll those protections back.

When I tell someone, in my smooth, trained voice, that I'm going deaf, they think, at first, that I'm joking. Ask a new friend, one chancing for the first time to trust you with a whispered confidence, to repeat that secret but louder. Misunderstand the volume of your own voice in public, because what's normal to you is obnoxious to others. I have one of those voices that carry—heads turn. Of course deafness made me ashamed. The strange thing would be if it hadn't.

I knew this feeling of old, of course, though not at this intensity: shame in the body, the shame of difference. When I returned to high school at fifteen the back of my head was shaved from neck to crown and adorned with an angry scar, a vertical slash that began at the topmost bulge of my vertebrae and ascended up. No one spoke to me about the scar directly, but I heard things. The muffled voice across the hall muttering, "John? You mean that weird-looking kid?" The girl who thought I was cute before the surgery was dating another boy. I didn't try to talk with many people until the hair had grown all the way back in. I internalized the discomfort. I didn't like the way I looked either, so of *course* I'd freak out the other kids.

I remained close to Jeff, though; he never judged me for being ill. Jeff had a car by then, and when we weren't breaking land-speed records in his Royal Monaco, I was making friends who didn't know me, or barely knew me, before the surgery. Our high school was big, and some of them hadn't even seen me without hair, or hadn't made the connection. Over time, the scar took on a different role. I didn't have to tell anyone about it. I never had to tell them. When I did choose to reveal it, it suddenly became an act of intimacy—I had control of who and when and how. If the conversation hit a lull, I'd lean over and say, "Check this out—run your finger right like this over the back of my head."

"Oh wow," one girl said as we drove out to Misquamicut beach in the summer of '93, using the grassy shoulder to pass other cars. I can remember how cold her hand was, and how I could feel it everywhere but that one ridge. "That is so cool. Did you almost die?"

When Elisa and I talked about marriage, prior to my getting sick, it was only to reaffirm that neither of us thought much of it. We'd been committed for years, called ourselves life partners, but didn't feel as though we needed a piece of paper to make it real. She'd never been one of those little girls who dreamed of weddings, and I was staggered to learn how much even the cheaper versions of such things cost. We'd agreed to let it be.

But then we cleared the dining room table and worked together to sort medical bills into sets by date, duplication, and where I was on my payment plans. As an adjunct professor, I worked without health insurance; Elisa's job offered benefits only to married partners. "We could get married," she said, "but please promise that if I get sick you'll take care of me too." She had reason to worry I wouldn't; things were dark in our relationship by then. My naked ears were too weak for phone voices most days, so I'd bark orders at Elisa from across the apartment: call the specialist back, take down a note to my work, call Norwich to see how Dad's surgery went. She had a job to report to—one she was lucky enough to perform from home—but when I was dizzy, she was my only outlet to the world.

In such an atmosphere did I enter the house with new hearing aids perched behind the outer shells of my ears. The volume control on the box around my neck would only work if I held it so close to the hearing aids that I couldn't make out the numbers. Quickly, I learned it by feel.

"Maybe you'll be one of those people who cry right away they're so happy," Elisa texted as I waited for the fitting. Here, at home, what struck me wasn't emotional relief but tumult. The refrigerator made noises like flying saucers in old movies. The cars outside were louder than surf on a loud day.

"Sweetie?"

"Yikes, let me turn these down."

"Can you hear me?"

"Hang on—don't talk for a minute."

"Sorry, I didn't know—"

"Gah! Hang on!"

By the time a few days had passed, I could manage to make out careful voices in quiet rooms, which is about what I'd been able to do before (loud rooms were impossible). I could also hear the rustle of fabric as though it sounded from behind my eyes. The phone, with some fussing, did work a little. I'd take walks to call family, muting the roar of the traffic.

"Hell-O!" Vivian's musical salutation. I guessed it was musical because I'd heard it so many times before. Now it came through as an indistinct vocal rustle and an open vowel that might have been any vowel.

"It's your lucky grandson!" I said. "Elisa and I are getting married."

"Well, I would think so. You've been living together five years."

"We're going to a judge. No big ceremony. Just picking a weekday and getting it done."

"That's best. Don't make a big deal about it."

Viv, prim and old New England, hadn't cared for E and I living together. "Sometimes you put your arm around her," she'd told me, "and it makes people uncomfortable. We've just been thinking of her as your roommate."

As it happened, May 9 was a good day—sound poor but vertigo abated. I dressed in a black suit over a purple shirt and Elisa emerged in a white dress with yellow flowers.

We'd decided to keep what was about to happen secret, letting our friends know only after the act was accomplished. Nursing a shared secret, making the most of the day, our mood picked up. No, I couldn't hear the woman at the Denver Office of the Clerk and Recorder, nor E's voice as she preceded me down the courthouse hall. But I could taste the champagne at Beast & Bottle and I could feel her hands in mine and I could hear the voice of the judge beside my ear when he read us our vows and prompted affirmation. Nervous, we fought back laughter until we began to tear up. I loved her for trusting me.

Elisa was brave that day. She'd met a healthy man of twenty-nine back in Boston, but she walked out of the Denver courthouse with a thirty-five-year-old she needed to financially support, at least for the time being. He was deaf and dizzy and he wore the badges of his disability for all to see. We couldn't whisper secrets, go out dancing, relax at parties, or see theater together anymore.

And our future was unpredictable. I might grow slow-witted before my time. Early dementia is troublingly common among those who lose their hearing in adulthood, but so is a milder lessening of competence, a drag in the mind.

There is a kind of learning psychologists call *incidental learning*: learning things you don't set out to learn. Children do this when they learn new words, picking up the meaning of phrases they've heard aloud but which haven't specifically been taught to them. Adults do it too. The way that four different people speak the name of a mutual acquaintance—little catches and tells in their voices—communicate something about what that person is like. Breath communicates: you know the friend who walks beside you is getting winded when they breathe a little faster; without consciously thinking about it, you slow your pace to let them recover. Things you aren't aware you've overheard come up in your own life and you're not in the dark about them. As I lost my hearing, I quit being able to distinguish breath, to hear little catches in the voice, to *over*hear.

In 2009, Brett Kemker et al., writing in the *Journal of the American Association of Audiology*, determined the reason so many accidents happen while drivers talk on their cell phones is because of our finite capacity for attention: "As visual tasks increase in difficulty, the effect of the auditory distraction is magnified." In the act of listening while impaired, pouring finite resources toward understanding someone's words means that you don't just hear less, you *see* less. Weaken one sense and the others fight harder for purchase. Deficit levies a tax.

If hearing aids worked as well as reading glasses, this wouldn't be much of a problem. Elisa's unaided vision is so impaired she's legally blind, but with contacts, she can see twenty-twenty. The trouble is, hearing aids aren't as good as that; they're not even close.

Downtown in a cold-weather city the week before Christmas. You snap a picture: glowing shops, a little snow along the curbs. Blue and green Christmas lights connect the streetlamps. Shoppers, bundled with bags, walk at leisure in the still air. There are cars but there's only a few, in the distance. Click.

The photo you've taken doesn't resemble what your eye took in. Instead, the headlights of a far-off car shine with shocking brightness, obscuring not only the car but the Christmas lights, the people passing, whiting out nearly everything but the back of that person beside you, which until now you hadn't realized loomed in the frame.

Better cameras and better photographers can improve on the picture, but hearing aids aren't so advanced. Someone calls to me on a street filled with evening traffic. If the cars are loud, the caller across the street can just raise her voice. But my hearing aids don't know what's more important: the traffic sounds or the person speaking. They make these two sounds into one sound. My ears, shorting out, perform less and less ably the task of deciphering human language. The machines help sound to get through, but speech is too delicate, too frangible.

The Widex aids I was fitted with compress the loudest sounds so they won't do me harm, like pushing down the peaks of a range of mountains. They amplify low sounds more than high ones. But they can only do so much. Healthy, unassisted ears can focus on important sounds while placing other, less important sounds in the background. Hearing aids—no matter how advanced or how expensive—can't entirely separate foreground from background. My Widex aids come equipped with microphones to pick up directional sound, but it's a clumsy switch, and one that only achieves so much.

As time passes, as the hearing aids become insepara-
ble from my sense of self, I'm coming to view the hearing
world with not resentment but confusion. How can it
be so easy? Hearing people laugh at a joke when I didn't
know words were spoken. They adjust themselves in
space without looking. They walk outdoors in the rain
without fear of their hardware getting wet. It's exotic to
watch them.

My sense of empathy misfires. I see a woman exit a
7/11 in the rain. *She'll get her hearing aids wet*, I think,
before catching myself. No, she doesn't wear them. She's
an able-bodied forty-something. Watching a movie, I'll
follow along as the main character tails the villain onto
a subway car. *Now he won't be able to hear for the background noise.* Worse: *Finally, he'll understand what it's like
for me.* But no; subways are loud, but they permit raised
speech, some understanding. They don't blot noise out
completely, not for everybody.

Some years back, a bunch of celebrities made YouTube
videos where they poured whole buckets of ice water on
their head to raise awareness of ALS. As I watched, I
kept panicking a little for their sake, thinking they were
destroying $6,000 worth of hearing aids. No, come back
to the real world—it's not like that, John.

Hearing aids work only up to a certain point. After
that, they're useless. One day my own ears will malfunc-
tion so badly I won't be able to make use of them. After
that, I'll get cochlear implants installed. Implants aren't
like real sound—for the majority of users, they're far
worse than real sound—so I can't help but dread the day.

When I could hear well, one of the sounds I most loved was a cat drinking water. A simple need was being satisfied for the cat, and the sound affirming that was satisfying for me. Similarly, there's a sound Elisa makes when she tastes something especially toothsome, a kind of satisfied smack of her lips. I missed hearing that when my ears went bad, but—before it happened—I didn't know it was a sound I'd miss.

Acquire a chronic condition and you'll feel like you're falling, or at least I did. Falling as if from a high cliff, coat whipping over your head, you lose the papers in your pocket. You lose Bach (the wind's too loud), but you don't land. You just keep falling.

Not long after I was fitted with hearing aids, Jeff moved to Falmouth, Maine. When Elisa and I traveled to visit him, he gave her a ride on his motorcycle ("I've never done that before!" she said, pulling her helmet off. "Is it always that fun?"). We drove out to DiMillo's in Portland for butter-broiled fish. As we waited for the check, Jeff told Elisa a story that got her laughing. I was too deaf to hear the story and didn't want to break in, so I distracted myself by reciting Sappho in my head. The writers change, but the habit's endured a quarter century.

In my eyes he matches the gods, that man who
sits there facing you—any man whatever—

> listening from closeby to the sweetness of your
>   voice as you talk, the
>
> sweetness of your laughter . . .

Another night, Jeff lit a fire, great clumps of snow coming down outside. Once the fire got low, he invited me on a walk through the Audubon preserve across the street. His wife, Maureen, a poet and an old friend, walks there every morning before work, regardless of weather.

"We won't be able to talk," he said as we laced up our boots to set out, "because the crunch of the snow will be too loud. So if you don't want to get your hearing aids wet, you should feel free to take them off."

The ground was covered, but moonlight worked behind the clouds like a bulb through a shade, and the white ground reflected that light. There were no birds, no people. Dogbane and arrowwood viburnum were only distinguishable by the shapes they made beneath the falling blanket. As we approached the banks of the Presumpscot, white of the air obscuring its farther shore, the water itself was frozen, the reach of it stretched to Casco Bay as flat as if sanded that way. On top of it fell a white torrent from the sky.

I heard the snow beneath my feet, and I heard Jeff's voice when he called out, "If you can hear what I'm saying, look where my finger's pointing now."

A farmhouse in the falling snow. Someone moving within.

On the Beach

The vertigo attacks settled into my head every other day by the autumn of 2013. When I could stand up and walk, I bought a cane. It looked clinical: gray foam and metal. My friends asked whether that was the only cane my insurance would pay for. What they didn't know is that insurance didn't pay for anything—I bought the cheap cane because Walgreens was the closest place that sold them and because the height was adjustable. When I turned thirty-seven on November 18, Elisa got me a nicer cane, mahogany.

"Only for when you need it," she said. "Only for now, until they can figure out what's wrong."

She gave me Jennifer Michael Hecht's book against suicide, but I couldn't bring myself to read it. "It's about why *not* to do it," she said. "It's about why you shouldn't."

I had quit teaching by then, quit driving a car. Elisa had spent her own days telecommuting at nearby coffee shops the prior semester so she could chauffeur me to class, sometimes walking me as far as the classroom door so I didn't fall over, but she couldn't keep it up. Her own job—editing for a tech company in Boston—was increasingly busy and, hand in glove with that, increasingly lucrative. I was mortified to be so crippled and dependent in what ought to have been my best working years. As my own bank account emptied and my debt increased, Elisa came to assume a larger portion of the household bills. I knew I had to get well as much for her sake as my own.

Sometimes she'd fly back east for a meeting while I lay in bed in Denver, feeling as alone as I'd ever felt. My mind kept itself busy through the vertigo—the sensation of falling through what at times felt like total deafness— by wondering how I would kill myself if it didn't stop by morning.

Getting into the bathtub with something sharp seemed the best course of action, letting my blood run out. Most days it felt like nothing more than a reassuring fantasy, something to calm me, the notion that there was a way out if I needed one. Other nights, as winter set in and I spent more and more of my time alone on my back, it was less of a fantasy—it felt urgent. I'd call the suicide hotline and couldn't make out what they said. I'd try to message them online, but my eyes couldn't focus enough to make out the words on the screen. (The deafness takes your ears; vertigo takes your eyes.)

Even if I'd been able to talk to them, I'd have been circumspect. Chatrooms warned me the whole thing was a trick, to get me to confess I had the intention and the means. As soon as I fessed up, they'd lock on my signal and send an ambulance or fire truck. The last thing I wanted to see was a rush of cops.

On March 24, 2004, the *Honolulu Star-Bulletin* ran a story beginning with, "A woman suffering from a rare disease apparently killed her children and herself." Subheaded "Meniere's Disease" [sic], the article goes on to describe how Jo Anna Miranda left a note before starting the fire and how she'd become increasingly desperate when no doctors were able to treat the strange noises in her ears. In a subsequent article, someone described as a "longtime family friend" goes on to plead: "If anyone in your family is affected by this disease, please be with them, please have the patience, please have the love." Later: "It comes on slowly and gradually and it got to the point, like in this case, where no one can handle ..."

The reporter cut him off there. *Where no one can handle* ... This terrified me, but so did the skirl in my head. Suicide was desperate but felt altruistic. I tried to explain to Elisa, and then to other friends, how my absence from the picture would brighten it. How I wasn't doing anyone any good here. I could see that what was wrong with me was taxing her. I felt like a prisoner of my own bed, or of the futon in my home office, where I spent sleepless nights and sick days when the ceiling wouldn't stop spinning and the roar wouldn't quit inside my head.

"I can't work. I can't even look at a screen," I'd tell her on the afternoons when I hadn't collected myself.

"Don't you think I'd be destroyed by that?" she said. "Don't you think I'd blame myself?"

"Of course you would. But you'll be heartbroken if I stay like this. I *can't* stay like this. *How* can I stay like this?"

Her nerves were frayed. Like me, she felt as though time had been reduced to a series of short highs and long sloughs. She'd walk me out of an appointment with a neurologist or audiologist or a tech taking MRIs. I'd shuffle with my cane as she tried to charm my chaos into calm.

"We'll call that new doctor as soon as we get home," she'd say, meaning whatever additional specialist we'd been referred to, palmed off to. One specialist suggested the House Ear Clinic in Los Angeles.

"It's a real Dr. House!" She said. "Maybe he'll figure it out!"

I wanted to keep things cheerful, but my head felt bare and full of echoes. Construction noises amplified in the hearing aids—I didn't know where they were. I hadn't slept for three nights for vertigo, just a few hours in the afternoon. I couldn't drive myself anywhere, couldn't walk far with the cane. Spinning was bad enough but pain came with it, and roaring. I couldn't hear music. I had too much time to think.

"He said celebrities go to the House Clinic. Maybe we'll see Ryan Adams there. You think maybe Ryan Adams will be there?" She'd try a tentative smile—would jokes work? "You have to be patient. There's an answer and someone will find it."

. . .

If directing *The Designated Mourner* had been a hobby, I'd have quit. But I wasn't teaching anymore, I'd gone on leave from the book review site I helped to run, and I'd quit writing. *The Designated Mourner*, our three-person play, was the only part of the external world I could touch and change. We'd canceled the last two rehearsals because I was throwing up from vertigo, but tonight I was doing all right. I listened, helped by the hearing aids, while Elisa read her part. Her character, Judy, was part of a small group of intellectuals in a country going authoritarian. In the first act of the play, the poor, the "dirt eaters," rise up; in the second act a far-right cabal puts them down. Judy's father, Howard, sympathizes with the poor, and because of it he's beaten, jailed, and killed. Judy's husband, Jack, abandons her and Howard to save his own ass.

Elisa's character had given up on life. She resented Jack—of course she did—for leaving her. But she also pitied him, because he was so pathetic, and because they had a history.

"Meanwhile," Elisa read on, "some awful trick of the night or the mind made me remember him as he'd been once—his confidence, the warmth, the directness of his touch."

"You're too distant," I told her. "You're reading like you're talking from the moon."

I'd directed a few plays by then, but I'd never directed someone I was so close to. Elisa was hurt by the notes I gave her. She thought I was being extra hard on her to prove to Aaron, a real actor, I knew how to direct.

"There's not enough on the page," she said. "The character's not fully written enough."

Aaron pushed his teacup a little forward, pulled it back.

"Don't read it like you're reading poetry at a poetry reading," I kept on. "You're just talking. This is happening for the first time. Remember, you've never said these words before."

"I think what John is saying," Aaron told her, "is that it's much more interesting to see an actor make a discovery onstage than to have them just recite something they know. So as you're saying all these words, you're discovering them too."

"Okay," Elisa said, "but these lines have a very *written* feel. Yours actually sound like you're thinking them."

Aaron carried about him the coy reserve of a strong personality in check. "Listen," he said, as though he was discovering the advice for the first time. "Play love first."

Aaron's tone was more even than mine. Half of a director's job is just to keep the wheels greased. When I gave Elisa notes, they would freeze her up. Aaron knew what he was doing.

"Always play love first," he went on. "It's always much more compelling when the first choice you make with another character is that you love them. I'm always going to choose first that I love Judy. Everything else comes second. Always remember that you love him. It makes everything interesting."

It was better advice than I'd ever given an actor. I'd been picturing Judy talking to her interrogators all the while. I'd pictured the audience as her judges at a trial, judges predetermined to find her guilty.

"I figured this out when I was doing *Much Ado About Nothing*," Aaron said. "Beatrice and Benedict don't work as characters unless they love each other from the start."

Elisa poured herself red wine from the open bottle. "Is Benedict the Keanu Reeves character?"

"That's Kenneth Branagh. He probably gave Keanu the Don John part because it has the fewest lines."

"Have you heard people pronounce that *ado* like 'goodbye'?" Elisa felt better. "They say, *Much Adieu About Nothing. Without further adieu.*"

Elisa notices small language things. I like pun jokes but she makes better ones. Lying in bed, she'll say, "Who's a pickle's favorite old-time comedienne?"

I guess, "Phyllis Diller?"

"Actually Dillis Diller."

Elisa, like me, like Aaron, does her best to dance light on her feet while she's poised, always, above a gulf of emotion. That was our idea for the play too—to play the characters as forcefully breezy, always afraid of letting the conversational ball drop. Because, were that ball to drop, it wouldn't stop falling.

Nearly everyone dies: murder, murder. Jack is the play's only survivor. He adapts in the way he has to adapt. He's got fight in him. I wished I had more fight.

One night alone in a hotel, Jack rationalizes abandoning his wife by rejecting the idea of the self:

And so what is it supposed to *mean* to me if someone tells me that the trousers I'm wearing were
worn "yesterday" by a man with my name, a man
who did this, a man who did that, or that they'll
be worn "tomorrow" by a man who is going to be
doing something or other? It all means exactly
nothing to me, because none of these people actually exist.

Like Jack, I was struggling with that famous problem,
the *mind-body problem*. Was the mind itself the body, was
the mind something else? And the soul? Sitting there
in what should have been a quiet room, pain in my left
ear like deep-sea pressure, I saw very nakedly that the
body and the mind, or the soul, were one and the same.
Not that the soul invented the body, but that the body
invented the soul. The self is the body. I thought of those
old pulp novels from the nineteenth century with titles
like *A Most Bloody and Cruel Murder, Committed on the
Body of Mrs. Elizabeth Wood* . . . titles that implied it was
not possible to murder the soul. But you *could* murder the
soul, of course you could. You could sicken it unto death.
We didn't know what was wrong with me, didn't know if
it was potentially fatal or what it would do as it worked
its course. But I didn't want to find a cure to recover my
body alone, my body as something external. My mind—
my soul—felt sick.

. . .

Like Jack and Judy in the play, Elisa and I came together over poetry. 2006: we met at a summer party in Quincy, decamped it for bourbon, and wound up reciting poems at each other for much of the night. Elisa was and is a brilliant poet. I was better at reading the stuff than writing it, but that's all the more reason to fall in love with a poet.

On our first real date we went to a poetry reading. (Years later, when the story came up, Elisa appraised it as "not even a date—you were just like, *There's this thing, and I'll be there, and maybe you'll be there too.*") Afterward, a group came back to my place. I offered Elisa scotch but she explained that it tasted like Band-Aids, so we drank bourbon with my friend Golaski and talked about spirituality. Golaski was stepping away from Catholicism, after a long ambivalence. "One thing I can't seem to let go of," he said, "or, rather, a question I keep asking, is the idea of the numinous. I do feel that there's something— *some* controlling force—but the idea that it's a man in the sky, or that we know his name—"

"I know exactly what you mean," I cut in. "I know *exactly* what you mean. When I was a kid, in the woods, the wind in those trees—you have the sense there's huge forces, even huge questions you just can't get a handle on."

Elisa asked what *numinous* meant. I said it was a pretentious way of saying *spiritual*. She rolled her eyes. "The *wind in the trees!*"

She smirked at me. I liked this. I liked being challenged.

"John's right," Golaski said. "I think it's New England. I think it's just being in the woods—both of us grew up on the edge of the woods. You walk in there and it feels dangerous."

"You weren't in *danger* in Con*nect*icut," Elisa said.

"*That's* numinosity!" I said or shouted. "Numinosity can make you feel endangered when you're safe. It puts your soul in peril."

Golaski was drinking and nodding. "The trees are a cathedral."

"I think," I said, "that maybe you just didn't feel it in El Paso because it's the desert." Elisa grew up in El Paso. My impression of El Paso resembled the landscape of roadrunner and coyote cartoons. "It's kind of pitiless, right?"

Golaski put his head back in the chair. "You feel the numinous *more* when it's pitiless."

"Are you *crazy*," she said. "People feel spiritual all the time in the desert. Haven't you ever heard of *the mystique of the desert?*"

"And you don't feel awe?" I said. "If you don't like numinosity let's go with awe. Do you ever feel awe in the desert?"

Elisa paused in a way I'd later come to see as characteristic. She was thinking about how to best get an idea across, figuring how to phrase it. It was a pause that set her listener at attention.

"Look, I think the desert's beautiful. But I'm an atheist. A thing can be beautiful without God being involved."

"*Not* God," I said. "*Awe.* Do you feel awe in the desert? A connection to things you can't understand, can't possibly understand?"

She paused again. Golaski rose and patted his pocket for his keys. I'd kiss Elisa the second I heard Golaski start his car.

She spoke slowly. "Obviously, there's a lot I don't understand, but I think it's just because I don't understand it, not because I can't."

I said, "I feel like all the poetry I love is about the numinous."

"Poemy poems about stones," she called the stuff I liked, as I rose to hug Golaski goodbye.

When he started his car, I did kiss her.

Late in 2013 we entered the terminal at LAX, hopeful. Elisa pretended to be startled by a giant poster of a lemur at the zoo and her alarm made the menace playful, the menace that shadowed us anyway. Leaning on her shoulder, I gestured with my cane at the unremarkable passengers-in-waiting with their sweatpants and their overstuffed duffels. "It's all so glamorous."

Elisa said, "Have you seen any celebrities yet?"

We took a cab to a hotel by the airport where she settled down with work emails and I closed my eyes. The noise in my ears was unusually loud that night. I tried to play white noise on headphones, but I couldn't make them loud enough. I took an Ambien. Two hours later, still awake, I took another. I may have hallucinated—I remember attempting to read *Gulliver's Travels* with a flashlight—Jonathan Swift had bad ears too—but the words didn't make sense and there seemed to be gold tracing between the letters.

The noise in my ears confused my doctors because it came and went, like my hearing itself, like the dizziness and the pain. Vertigo comes and goes, of course: that's what vertigo is. But tinnitus shouldn't shift like this.

"Does it get worse before the vertigo begins?" doctors asked me. I said sometimes yes, sometimes no. But I got the sense they didn't hear me, not precisely. Or, rather, they didn't mind about the "sometimes no" part, because it didn't accord with diseases on file.

The first time I heard the phrase *Ménière's disease* was at the Massachusetts Eye and Ear Clinic, about a year after Elisa and I first met. I'd had a pair of vertigo attacks—my first—within a week of each other, and although I wouldn't have traced the problem to my ears, my doctor referred me to an otologist. The word comes from the Greek *otos*—ears. I took the train to Charles/MGH and took a hearing test and waited to learn what was wrong.

The doctor shook my hand with an easygoing, commanding assurance and told me I probably had Ménière's disease, which meant "your ears are like a beat-up old car that runs good on some days, and other days doesn't run good at all. Eventually, the engine won't ever run."

Did that mean I would lose all of my hearing? How soon?

"There's no way to predict it. Maybe yes, maybe no. Avoid salt. That pepperoni pizza? Maybe give it a pass."

On my own, on the Mayo Clinic website and some chat rooms and Wikipedia, I discovered that Ménière's is a diagnosis of exclusion, meaning if you're subject to vertigo attacks and tinnitus, and your ability to hear worsens with time (dipping first for the low tones, then the high), and there isn't anything *else* identifiably wrong with you . . . well, then we may as well call it Ménière's. There's nothing else to call it. The condition—such as it is, remains vastly overdiagnosed. Fifty years from now it will be ten conditions, each with a different prognosis. Some will involve pain in the ears and some won't. Some will resolve over time and others will progress.

Over weeks of emailing doctors, calling in a second opinion, then a third, I learned there's no reliable test for Ménière's, no reliable treatment, and no consensus on its cause. Low-salt diets and diuretics may help to prevent attacks, but few studies support their effectiveness. Regular steroidal injections through the drum of the ear possibly reduce the frequency of vertigo, but they won't do anything for the ringing in your ears or the loss of your hearing. Repeated injections have been known to damage the ear, often badly. They don't work for everyone. They didn't work for me.

What really damages your ears is destroying their function completely with the antibiotic gentamicin. This is a last resort doctors have turned to when the vertigo is unremitting—when it literally never stops. They will not use it, however, if the patient has trouble with both ears, which I did. In such situations, few options remain, save the search for a new treatment, a more specific diagnosis.

When Jonathan Swift had the condition, at least one doctor blamed it on eating too many apples. Sweetness cloys the brain to madness. Medicine, at least based on the PubMed articles I was reading, had not advanced leaps in the last three hundred years, at least not in regards to Ménière's.

And for a while, back in Boston, it hardly mattered: my hearing was fine. There was a little roaring in one ear or the other on odd days, but nothing extravagant. I had vertigo attacks without much warning but they didn't happen often, maybe once a month. I took a Valium or a Dramamine and it passed.

Only when we moved to Colorado did the life I had built, or was trying to build, collapse from the weight of the thing in my head. The symptoms grew stronger. New doctors told us they *would* have favored Ménière's as a diagnosis, but there were complications. The typical Ménière's patient—to the extent such a person exists— maintains relatively stable hearing levels over short periods of time. I didn't. My hearing came and went by the hour. The typical Ménière's patient experiences no fluctuation in hearing outside of discrete vertigo attacks. I wasn't typical.

I let them pierce my eardrums and tap my spine. After several protracted days of vertigo, I asked Elisa to drive me to the emergency room. They sent me home.

Elisa and I held hands in the waiting room at House Ear Clinic outside Beverly Hills. We had arrived with time to spare. I filled out the paperwork with an unsteady hand.

Neither of us could calm ourselves to read. My thoughts leapt around but didn't make solid shapes.

The specialist entered the examination room as confident as I've ever seen a man. He looked in my eyes, in my ears, he asked me questions.

"Do loud sounds especially bother you?"

"Sometimes."

"Have you been treated for ear infections?"

"As a kid. Long ago."

"Okay. Okay, I think we can get you fixed up."

I was led to a larger room where a technician fed a tube into my nose with a tiny camera on its end, fishing for data. The specialist suspected a crack in the hard bone that protects the ear. We tested for it. We also tested for a hole in the tiny ducts that carry fluid from one part of the ear to another. I was too strung out by then to remember the details of the tests, only that I had to sit very still and think my thoughts, which were not thoughts but fears.

"We've ruled out superior canal dehiscence and we've ruled out the perilymph fistula," the specialist said when we met again in his office. He looked over the chart for a moment in silence, then wheeled his chair to face me.

"You are welcome," he said, "to come and see me anytime. But I don't think I can be of any further help in diagnosing what's affecting you."

I couldn't get my head around it. I said nothing.

"I am recommending a rheumatologist. I don't think this is Ménière's disease to the extent that I'm familiar with it, but see if you can get an appointment while you're still in town. She'll take good care of you."

I asked him to clarify—should I come back to see him after I'd talked with this other doctor?

He didn't shake his head, but he did sigh a little.

There was a car-sized model of the human ear outside the clinic. I stared at its coin sack of a cochlea while Elisa called the rheumatologist. Could we come back in two months? Trying not to feel defeated—we both tried hard—we climbed into the rental car and drove to Santa Monica, talking about how of course it had to be an autoimmune condition, of course it did. We traded miracle-cure stories about people we knew with autoimmune problems, or people we'd just heard talked about. I knew the drill now—two months spinning in the dark would pass a little easier than last time. And hey, we'd get to come to LA again. I still had a line of credit. Once I was cured, I could work three times as hard. I could get the corporate kind of job I used to have before I started teaching, the kind of job that pays a living wage. We would be okay.

After dinner we sat on the beach and watched the sun dab its pinks. Everyone stopped to watch: kids with sunburns, waiters in pressed shirts, tourists with Leicas, locals with Leicas; in between them, outnumbering them, sat the people who lived on the beach. I'd been to Santa Monica before, and like everyone I noticed all the homeless residents ringed with worn-out shopping bags and surplus blankets. The swollen ankles of sick livers. Their fate keeps the rest of the country tapping keyboards and running cards with grim smiles on our faces. I wanted to talk with them. But I couldn't understand strangers' voices the way I used to. I felt too self-conscious.

Suicide may be a cruelty to those around me, but I saw it as a kindness: they wouldn't have to watch someone they loved fall irreparably apart. I might wake up totally deaf tomorrow, throwing Elisa into a three-month confusion of cochlear implants, a hundred slow walks from the car to the clinic, prematurely aging us until we naturally aged in place. My vertigo might become intractable, something she couldn't manage on her own; I didn't want her to pay for my convalescence, or make my mother waste her retirement years looking after me. To dismiss suicide was to give fate more rein, to give up what small power I still had against the course of my life.

And so the urge to get to know the people who lived on the beach was selfish: one way of breaking through this haze of feeling so worthless would be to come to understand other people whose own lives had fallen apart; my human sympathy would warm, and I'd come to see that if the lives of the broken had value, intrinsic value, my own life might too, because, after all, wasn't I part of humanity? The phrase *fellow creature*, and the tenderness of that phrase applied to me too, no? Self-pity is not contemptable in a sane world, not when it keeps you from killing yourself. In any case, I've never felt guilty when I pitied someone else—they're entitled to your tenderness. Aren't you entitled to a tenderness of your own measure, a self-indulgent tenderness?

Instead, I was cruel to myself and to everyone else, because the world was cruel (like the father in a book—I can't remember which book—who beats his deaf son because, "He has to learn that what he does not hear, he will *feel*").

We didn't have enough pity for one another. The woman on my left with the matted dreads and the seven layers of makeup: why was she consigned to a life outside society while rich criminals redecorated neo-Palladian estates in Trousdale? You could walk to Trousdale from here. And yet by no higher order than mere chance, she was left alone and Trousdale Man was ensconced in fripperies.

Tourists surged past me, and shopkeepers and the thoughtful retirees of this town, all their eyes averted from the homeless. There is no squaring pity: we're invisible to one another *because* of self-sympathy. And yet that self-sympathy keeps us sane. My thoughts were a mess about this, my feelings were a mess. I wanted to keep from monologizing to Elisa about it like I had on nights before. I vowed to myself we'd talk about the play instead, about life.

In his 1906 novel of mountain travel, translated by Alan Turney as *The Three Cornered World*, Natsume Sōseki's narrator floats down the Ōi River toward Yoshida and muses to himself:

> If you stood on the approach to the Nihonbashi bridge in Tokyo, which hundreds of people cross every minute, and were able to elicit from each individual that went past what turmoil and confusion lay buried in his heart, you would find yourself bemused by the knowledge of what this world can do to a man, and life would become unbearable.

I wanted to stay on this beach until nothing scared me. Elisa pulled me to my feet. I followed to the car.

At the hotel, Elisa and I were careful not to talk about the clinic. She lay in bed reviewing her lines.

I said, "I love how Aaron can mix registers, as an actor I mean. He's so mild mannered in real life. Where does he get all that emotion from?"

Elisa looked pained. "You compliment Aaron all the time. But you never compliment me. You're always like *aaa ooo eee, here's what you're doing wrong.*"

I defended myself: "He's been acting for twenty years."

"You're not listening."

"Sure I am."

"No, you're not."

"I'm right here, I'm listening."

"No, you're *not*, because I've been saying this all *year*: I'm saying I want you to believe in me."

I kept thinking I had. I kept thinking I'd said it. How could I pay attention to the feelings of others? In the state I was in, all I could do was not walk into traffic. Fuck the drivers.

"Look," I flailed my arms. "I'm *sorry* I can't be more sensitive. I'm—I'm going through some stuff right now."

"*I'm* going through it *with* you," she said. "I've been going through it with you the whole time. It wouldn't kill you to be nice to me."

She was hurt. I said I knew she'd been there for me all

the while and I felt guilty about it. I wanted to get well and buy a new suit and make some money so she could write poem after poem. I didn't feel like myself; I wanted the way I felt not to *be* myself.

"Then try not to be so *impatient* with me. You yell at me. Like if you need me to make a phone call for you, you say *do it right now.* You yell at me if I can't do it right away."

It ended in the best way, as our talks often did, with me stroking her hair and apologizing. We have a private language designed to soothe, much of which has to do with the proposition that Elisa is, in fact, a cat, one very dear to me. We talked about this until we were both calm. I put my arm around her and she set her head against my chest.

She said, "Don't you think I'd be lonely without you?"

She said, "That rheumatologist has an office in Beverly Hills. Rich people get all the good doctors."

She said, "Why is a pickle container never completely closed?"

On the night we were set to perform the play at Lighthouse—a writing center in an old mansion on Capitol Hill in Denver—I busied myself with my headphones in the office we were using as a greenroom. I had a small acting role in the performance, and I like to zone out before I act. Since college I'd readied myself by playing some Gavin Bryars on headphones, a little ritual.

Bryars is a minimalist composer who sometimes makes pieces that sound fourteenth century. They're often old mandolin things he's set for cello and strings. These particular settings, *Oi me lasso*, are full of cathedral echoes. It settles my pulse, relaxes me the way petting Elisa's hair relaxes me. It allows me to hold a single thought in my head at once.

But I couldn't get it loud enough to distinguish. If you picture sound waves as mountains, I could hear only the summits, incoherent without the rest. As I fussed with the controller, the sounds thinned out and distorted.

I knew Elisa was speaking but I couldn't make out the words.

"Are you speaking loudly or quietly?"

"Normal."

Aaron: "Listen John, we know your cues. We can just kick your legs under the table if you miss them. Right, Elisa?"

How could this be the same world as the one I woke into, the one where it seemed as though my ears would be okay for the day? To Aaron and Elisa it looked the same—they didn't even *think* about their ears. They didn't walk into rooms and panic at the acoustics, or get spooked by a sound of rubbing inside their heads, one that would steal low tones from them any moment. They didn't feel that sick feeling when you're sitting two feet from a voice you didn't know had been speaking, a voice that sent the room into action, got heads nodding, your head the only head that didn't nod, your head the only one stuffed with cotton, one-fifth dead to the music of reality, the shuffles and scrapes that swayed listeners the way wind sways trees.

We walked upstairs. As soon as we joined our audience, Aaron boisterously went around shaking hands. "Hi, I'm the designated mourner. Good to meet you, I'm the designated mourner."

Like that, the play began. The characters soliloquize most of the time, only sometimes addressing each other, correcting each other or falling over each other's lines, the way couples do when they tell the same story.

At one point, Elisa and Aaron, a couple in crisis, argue about what went wrong, and Aaron bangs the table. He banged it hard that night, shouting, "Jesus Christ, will you stop bothering me?" Elisa started crying. We hadn't rehearsed that.

I heard my cue, delivered my line, and disappeared downstage during intermission. My character doesn't appear in the final act. When I returned, an hour later, the applause had died down and the room was a chaos of conversation. Aaron and Elisa circulated. Smiling attendees shook their hands.

A woman I didn't know approached me and started talking. Later, I learned she was the arts editor at our local public radio station. I couldn't understand her. I took my hearing aids out, thinking I'd be spared the echoes, but I still couldn't understand her—she was too faint. I leaned in, cupped my ear, felt tired. I heard Elisa laugh, the laugh she laughs when she's really happy: that sound cut through the cloud, and so I moved in her direction. I couldn't hear what Elisa said either, even when I asked her to shout, lean in and shout, really shout.

One after another, new people approached me and moved as though they were praising the play. If I was lucky enough to catch a stray word, I made a general statement about that word and hoped it counted as conversation. I pointed to my ears, apologized. I stood there in the warm burble of inaudible voices and shook my head. It went on like that a long time.

The Polar Vortex

Once the nurse had my clothes off and had positioned
me on a gurney at the entrance to a man-sized toaster, she
began to sprinkle me with powder, beige stuff, face to toes,
then smoothed it in like you would a dry rub. My hearing
aids were tucked in a locker. I felt panicked without them.

"*Everything* off," she'd repeated, directing me to
the changing closet. This clarified the role of the hear
ing aids: they were an appurtenance only, nonessential.
They weren't like the cow membrane I'd needed to have
grafted to my spine as a teen, or the titanium bar fastened onto the bones of my wrist after a fall. They didn't
make me transhuman. They could be broken with ease,
lost or taken.

I stared up at the nurse. The fluorescent light didn't
silhouette her. It was a clinical light in a white room, but
the sterility of the place was necessary. If I wanted a cure
for this thing that had happened to me, I had to diagnose
it first, and diagnosis required all-white rooms.

She said, "You'll be able to wash the powder off later. With luck, it will have changed color by then."

The change in color of the powder would be accomplished—or not—by heat. Heat that would emanate from the toaster, a walk-in box adorned with tinfoil and bare joints.

The nurse—I never got her name—wore gloves as she dusted me, the powder less coarse than I imagined before it covered my skin.

I felt like a pharaoh on the slab, being rubbed with natron salt before I was wrapped. Tense, I tried a joke. I had trouble hearing my own voice so I talked in a bar voice.

"Is that thing going to pop me out the top when I'm done?"

She gave me a look that implied she'd heard every joke a naked man can make and hadn't cared for one of them.

"So, okay, so you wheel me into the machine and then what happens?"

She kept her eyes on the spots where my torso connected with the gurney. She'd missed them in her first pass.

"Then we test the brain's response to heat."

"My whole nervous system, though, right? The autonomic pathways?"

"Well!" she said, as though that were the last word. "I guess you've already read about it."

I'd only scanned Wikipedia on my phone in the waiting room. I still didn't understand the powder.

"It turns purple," she said, "if you sweat right."

She was correct: I did end the afternoon on the purple side; emerging from the toaster, I resembled a 6'4" bruise, or maybe a carnival dancer. But that was still to come. As she worked the powder up around my ears, I asked, "What sort of diseases would make me *not* turn purple?"

"Oh," she said, as though putting the subject to bed now for good, "all kinds of things."

Medical personnel are very good at explaining things in either the simplest or the most complex possible terms, but little in between. Jargon has a lot to do with this, but so does a vague contempt for patients that develops as a by-product of guarding yourself against emotional collapse. If you don't have time to cry about everything, you wind up compensating with a roll of your eyes.

There's an additional reason for all those zero-to-sixty explanations, though. It's one we hesitate to talk about because we actively fear it. But that doesn't make it less real. Often, doctors and nurses and technicians, medical journals and studies and pop science, are bad at explaining things because the embarrassing truth is that none of them understand what's really going on. Around certain diseases, particularly those of diagnostic exclusion— diagnoses unverifiable through tests—there exists a hearty portion of bluffing. Whatever was wrong with my ears or brain or nerves—whatever caused me to collapse and the world to spin around me, caused all external sound to disappear without warning, and take on a jet-engine roar only I could hear—was one of these mystery conditions, the kind no one wants to admit being baffled by.

Consequently, I saw a fair bit of bluffing at the Mayo Clinic. No one shocks as readily as a cynic, so of course I was shocked by it.

"What kind of music do you want in the chamber," the nurse asked, removing her beige-powder gloves.

"Whatever you play I probably won't hear too well. So, just play your favorite."

She wheeled me into the device. Through a window to my right I watched her manipulating dials. Just then, as the red bars lit above me and my skin began to prick the way skin does on a hot, beachy day, I heard music coming faintly from a speaker above.

It dawned on me I ought to have said, "Play anything except for Frank Sinatra." But there it was:

Come fly with me!
Let's fly, let's fly away.

The toaster test turned out to be something called a thermoregulatory sweat test, one that measures the body's response to heat: if your skin doesn't warm in the proper pattern, then your nervous system might be damaged. My nervous system appeared to be functioning well, but I didn't know that when I landed at the Rochester, Minnesota, airport three days before. I didn't want to test positive in a nerve damage test per se, but I wanted to find a test that diagnosed me, either curing me or putting a name to whatever was wrong.

The Mayo Clinic has a reputation. "They'll fix you up," old friends assured me before my visit. Every time my courage began to falter in the run-up, Elisa would say, "Just wait and see what Mayo says." This confidence is at least two generations old. According to Leonard Berry and Kent Seltman's *Management Lessons from Mayo Clinic*, polling respondents in 1961 were already referring to the Mayo Clinic as "a court of last resort—the 'Supreme Court' of Medical Opinion." More recently, in a national survey from 2007, respondents were asked "what healthcare institution they would choose for themselves or a family member if insurance or finances would permit them to go anywhere." Mayo Clinic was mentioned more than twice as frequently as anyplace else.

But the particularities of visiting Mayo aren't the sort of things people think about until they get sick. At the time of my visit—early 2014—Mayo's website advised prospective patients to expect a week-long stay. Such a stay would cost hundreds before travel was factored in. And I couldn't travel alone. My new marriage to Elisa meant I now had health insurance to pay for the visit, but it came with a $2,000 deductible. I was working less, earning less thanks to the mystery illness, but Elisa couldn't make the trip; my mother saved the day, offering not only to fly there along with me but to pay for both of our flights and our hotel. I agitated through the nights on the week leading up to the journey, away from Elisa, in Connecticut's post-Christmas fade, while my mother worried over what warm clothes to pack. Then we flew north, straight into the cold.

Rochester knocked together an airport early last century for near-exclusive use by patients of Mayo Clinic. While Mayo directly employs only a third of Rochester residents, most of the rest work in subsidiary jobs: long-stay hotels, meals, transportation, and a city government that takes its marching orders from HQ. It's the kind of relationship with a single employer you don't see much in midsize cities anymore. Rochester is a company town.

Timing, as usual, was everything: the post–Civil War decades were boom years for clinical breakthroughs and the brothers Mayo were smart enough to understand what was happening around them. The germ theory of disease was only then coming into common practice, and so the Mayos were relatively unique in their insistence on sterile theaters. Thanks to chloroform, patients and surgeons were no longer made to endure what Fanny Burney described in 1811 as the "unavailing wretchedness" of procedures without anesthetic. In the early years of that century, following a partial mastectomy, Burney, still weeping in postsurgical agony, wrote to her sister describing what the nightmare had been like:

> I then felt the Knife tackling against the breast bone — scraping it! — This performed, while I yet remained in utterly speechless torture . . . I then saw my good Dr Larry, pale nearly as myself, his face streaked with blood, its expression depicting grief, apprehension, & almost horror.

The trenches of World War I and the Spanish flu presented entirely novel horrors, and in the wake of a rush of patients to Rochester, the brothers Mayo fell upon a new idea: a clinic of salaried physicians, the first anywhere of its kind, and a principal of organization that would make their family name into what Berry and Seltman call "one of the most influential and valuable service brands in the world."

Valuable here is a charged word, in that the value so many pilgrims place on a journey to Mayo often consists not only of money they've saved or borrowed but of their own continued existence. The value can be life itself.

As we taxied in on arrival, I switched my phone out of airplane mode. A long row of weather alerts appeared, their tone increasing in alarm as we rushed through the cold to our long-stay hotel. *Meteorologists recommend no more than three minutes' exposure to the cold . . . try to travel in groups . . . always let someone know where you are . . . only go outdoors if you cannot possibly avoid it . . .*

As I settled in over the next few days of my stay, what worried me about the cold was not the number of warnings, or even the feel of the air, it was the fact that even the locals seemed alarmed. As in Jack London's "To Build a Fire," spit *crackled* when it hit the snow. The wind wasn't hard—doors weren't obstinate—but there wasn't any part of your body that wasn't cold outdoors: shivers under your arms, stinging thighs, a blade at your back. Your body stiffened and resisted movement. Nobody walked outside, they ran. And nobody joked about the cold.

On arriving at our hotel, we passed a woman emerging with her partner, or her father, or her son? The hood and scarf she wore weren't the only reasons it wasn't possible to guess her age: disease had withered her, and it frightened me to see it. People close to death develop a certain look, a dazed extremis. Who knows what she looked like when she was well, maybe weeks before? I carried a suitcase in one hand and a bag in the other, and amazingly she remained at the hotel entrance to hold the door for me. I offered a smile, but a joke about the cold died in my throat. I didn't want to waste her time.

Where was she going now that clinic hours were through? Probably the same place my mother and I dashed to an hour later, after stowing our bags in a room that had seen more than its share of bad nights. We were planning on a boisterous late dinner at the Canadian Honker next door, but I didn't feel good. "How many people have died in this room, do you think? Or slept their last night?"

"Don't be so dark," my mother said. "Try to think of all the people who got a good night's sleep here once they knew they'd be cured."

Dinner, we decided, would cheer us both, and we managed to find seats just before the Canadian Honker's kitchen closed.

Cheese curds, it turns out, are just fried cheese. Expecting Mayo would be taking blood the next day, I asked about the liver and onions and was told people came from "miles around" to partake of it. I ordered the dish and grew convinced those miles-long travelers came only once.

On the space walk thirty feet to our hotel, and once my hearing aids were off and I was alone in bed with the roaring in my ears and with my thoughts, I tried to encourage myself about the week that lay ahead and to fight back fear. None of the doctors I'd seen so far had been able to help, but maybe someone at Mayo could.

Shortly before my pilgrimage to Mayo, I paid a visit to Yale, which wasn't all that far from my hometown. If someone there could help, I reasoned, I might be able to go back as often as I liked. I met with a highly recommended neurotologist (an expert on how the ear gets on with the brain) who suggested the trouble lay in what was missing: a pair of organelles called endolymphatic sacs. These turned out to be the tiny pouches which keep a reserve of excess fluid on hand, a set of dampeners, to modulate the moistness of the inner ear. Except, he said, that I didn't have them. Had they always been missing? "There's no way to test if this is why you're sick," he told me, "but that doesn't really matter because there's nothing we could do to treat it if we *could* prove it. So I'm . . . I'm just really, really sorry. But I wanted to offer a theory anyway. I wanted to offer you *some*thing."

Every otologist after that shook their heads at the idea. "You *have* endolymphatic sacs," they'd say, pointing at a white dot on a scan. "*There* they are." How would I know any better? I can find them in the otological anatomy books and I can see the white dots on the X-ray but I can't make the one correspond to the other.

Why had I imagined I'd find deliverance at the soft hand of a specialist? Specialists are only looking within a narrow range of possibilities. General practitioners, on the other hand, see all kinds of sickness. Maybe someone other than my usual GP would spot in a moment the very thing we'd all missed for so long. I looked for and located someone with good reviews.

It had been a long day for the GP when I arrived. He was gathering papers together when I entered. His consultation room was disheveled.

"What can I do for you?" He hardly looked at me. I guessed he was anxious to be home.

"Well, should I explain in detail? Or were you able to look at my records?" This was my standard opener. Because doctors generally gave no more than twenty minutes to patient visits, and because my history took some time to relate, I tried to send a summary and a timeline well ahead.

"No, I haven't. Can you just tell me briefly?"

Like most of the physicians I saw, he kept his eyes on the screen while I spoke. Years before, a neurologist I met at a party had told me, "Generally, we're able to figure out what's wrong about three minutes after you walk into the consulting room. If we can't figure it out by then, we probably won't." He went on to explain the checklist that must have been running through that GP's mind as he typed. "When you walk in there he's got a head full of potential diseases, and he's just narrowing them down and ticking them off."

"Checking boxes?"

"Unchecking boxes, yeah."

The GP introduced the idea of Ménière's disease as soon as I began to talk, but when I explained that my hearing fluctuated by the hour he shook his head. "This might be subjective . . ."

It wasn't my first open mic. I reached into the knapsack I carried from appointment to appointment and produced nine months' worth of hearing tests: a jagged line that dipped and ascended each visit; there was, at that time, no visible pattern to the changes. Since then, a pattern has appeared, one of falling—I have fewer good days. In fits and starts, my hearing is going away.

"All right, so how do you think I can help you?"

I understand this question better now than I did at the time. Here was a healer face-to-face with something he was almost certain he couldn't heal. Living with misfortune has made me belatedly sympathetic to characters like this overworked doctor.

In that office, amid the fluorescence, I wanted to seem more sober than usual, to set my hands together as if in prayer and say, "What I want should be obvious: I want a new idea. I want something for my health, in exchange for the copay and deductible, and the monthly cost of my insurance, and the debt. I need a suggestion of what to try next—anything. What I really want is my old life back. I want to teach and hike again, and to hear music again, and to go out to dinner in groups, and to hear on the bus. I want to walk in a straight line. And I want to not be afraid."

I delivered a milder version, and he shrugged and said, "I don't know." He looked at his watch. "We can meet again, but we're booking now about two months out."

"What would you do," I said, gently, "if you had to quit your job, couldn't drive, couldn't talk on the phone, and were always distracted, like Harrison Bergeron, by a blaring in your ears that never quit . . . what would your next step be?"

I had made him uncomfortable—I had wanted to—but he was professional. "Have you considered the Mayo Clinic?"

Why do we assume doctors can fix nearly anything? Why do we assume that even when cures aren't around now, they're around the corner, or a few years ahead? The cosmos is too big for us to understand, and the human body is too mysterious. Yet we fight on, visiting specialist after specialist, reading journal articles, signing up for drug trials.

Aside from the heroic work of TV doctors, the cause of our confusion—our drive to keep pushing until we're cured—probably lies with penicillin. The history of modern medical discoveries, and the public reaction they engendered at the time, may testify to penicillin's singularity, and why it's problematic as a general model. Contrast the speed of its acceptance with that of, say, vaccines, controversial—needlessly so, but nonetheless—long before the most recent pandemic. Eighteenth-century trials, like when Edward Jenner poked a needle into a cow pustule then jabbed it into a healthy human, seemed distasteful, and created an atmosphere of suspicion that has persisted. The science was anything but intuitive. Wouldn't taking a bit of sickness make you sick? (See James Gillray's 1802 illustration "The Cow-pock," in which the newly vaccinated sprout buboes of charging steer heads and hooves). Sanitation for cholera and the conquest of plague were preventative rather than curative and so appear in retrospect, while marvelous, impersonal. Penicillin is different. When you're sick, you're given a pill. You take it and you're cured.

Did I expect the Mayo Clinic would hand me a pill to make me better? Yes, a little. Had I been egged into this? The doctor, showing me to the door, merely put it that "Mayo offers team care. That's their model. So various specialists converse with each other to diagnose you collaboratively."

Why had I imagined a conference table? In the months leading up to my visit, I pictured a boardroom full of serious people sharing the monstrous packet of test notes I'd been carrying from office to office all year; I saw them putting questions to one another pointedly, even arguing, finally nodding in agreement. *Now let's get this man well.* But it isn't like that. All of what I'd fantasized about takes place (or doesn't) electronically: notes and test results are entered into Mayo's system by each physician and then consulted by the next in turn.

The efficiency of Mayo's system is one of the things that sets it apart. So is the size of its campus. We were awed on the first morning we darted from the cold into the main building's summery atrium. Passing us, on his way out the door, was a man with a purple tumor the size and shape of a Bartlett pear on his cheek, a permanent IV line protruding from its top like a stem. He smiled at us through the dazzling glass.

Everyone I met for that week would be within walking distance. This was significant because for months—incapable of making my own appointments over the phone (for privacy reasons, many doctors will not use email)—I'd relied on Elisa to place calls for me, arrange our travel, negotiate insurance. My mother wouldn't have such a burden on her hands—it was all here, all scheduled on our behalf. And she was beside me, still shivering from the blast outside, when my Mayo-assigned internist made his appearance.

It's the practice at Mayo to begin each visit by matching patients up with an internist who will examine, consult with, and then direct them to specific specialists. I was lucky in at least one portion of my visit in that the doctor they matched me with was by far the most pleasant and *present* of the people I'd meet in Rochester. This is not surprising. Internists often make their reputations on bedside manner; specialists do not.

"How was your trip?" he asked once we'd made ourselves comfortable in his office chairs.

"Cold," my mother said. "You're brave to live somewhere this cold."

He smiled. "My wife, this morning, used a different word."

I got busy explaining to him all I'd experienced the year before, how it had changed my life, and what seemed to set my own condition apart from the others I'd read about.

"My hearing comes and goes, comes and goes. Have you ever heard of something like this?"

He neither nodded nor shook his head. "Our specialists," he said, "very well may have."

"Odd things make a difference. For example, the symptoms often improve slightly after a glass of red wine."

He smiled again. "If you think you're the first to tell me that alcohol improves a neurological condition, you'd be mistaken."

We adjourned to a room beside the office to carry out an examination. After he'd looked me over and asked me the usual yes or no questions, we went back to his office and he started typing.

"I'm going to put you in for appointments with an ophthalmologist, an otologist, and a neurologist. Mayo doesn't accept most tests from other hospitals—we prefer to use our own—so I'll set you up for a number of those too. The specialists will order some as well. Ah." He clicked his keyboard. "Well, let's see, it looks as though otology's booking two months out."

My muscles jumped. "The website we saw, the Mayo site . . . it told us to plan for a week-long stay."

The doctor looked as though he'd bitten into something bitter. "That language is a pernicious lie. There can be long delays. I have told them what I thought of that language. But I'll tell the system what you need and we'll see if it can get you in sooner . . . oh, look at that, it just did. You'll collect your copy at the desk."

At the clinic's appointment desk, a quiet woman handed us each a ten-page packet listing each consultation and test over the next five days—our visit to otology would happen last, at the end of the week. Time spent traveling between floors of the Gonda Building was factored in, as were slight delays, typical test times, extended conversations. We were given beepers when we arrived at the appointed floor and then we did our best to get comfortable in the city-block-wide waiting room. We were never late.

Expensive art hung everywhere. Late Warhols lined the hall outside the cafeteria. A huge Chihuly chandelier loomed over the Gonda's lobby (donated by philanthropist Serena Fleischhaker, who hoped, rather ominously, that it would encourage patients to "raise their eyes toward the heavens.")

Clearly, this is designed to throw the visitor into a state of awe, particularly those highly paying overseas visitors: the sheikhs and the autocrat's spouses and children who fly in nightly. In my distressed mental state, I found the opulence obnoxious, but then what had I desired? Dimly functional rooms and anonymous corridors? I'd found enough of those at our long-stay hotel. The halls at the Aspen Suites, filled with sufferers, and our worn-in room also made me sad. Evenings there, I'd wonder at how many invalids also spent sleepless nights in that bed.

I wondered again who had died there. I wanted to know their names.

At night the roaring in my ears grew arrogant enough my mother's voice couldn't cut into it, even with my hearing aids turned up high. I would switch the TV loud and try to catch a word or two, anything. That's when I learned Fox News's real strategy: roping in older viewers as much by audibility as affiliation. Announcers on Fox spoke clearer and louder than they did anywhere else. As a consequence, at the Mayo Clinic I watched Bill O'Reilly every night. By 9 p.m., his was the only voice I could discern, his noxious razzmatazz the only human sound in the universe.

Mayo is fabulously big and intimidating, and my mother and I talked about how we couldn't help but feel minimized by the colossus we shuffled through. "They were no-nonsense," she said later. "I mean, you hear about Midwestern friendliness, and this wasn't it." Just like in other hospitals I'd visited, the medical technicians were cheerier than the doctors, but even with the medical technicians, conversations could cool to zero.

One technician at Mayo, during an otherwise-routine test, responded to my wandering thoughts about the life expectancy of Ménière's sufferers with "yeah, you know, a lot of people, they kill themselves."

On another occasion, three days into my Mayo visit, I waited nervously on an exam table in the vestibular department, ready for another test. This one was designed to measure my ears' ability to right themselves after medically induced dizziness. Ice water was prepared for

injection into my ears in order to unsettle the movement of my eyes. To read the results, I was fit with a
sort of blacked-out scuba mask, sending my visual field
into darkness. There, a laser would track my eyes as they
regained function. The longer they took, the more the
vestibular canals in my inner ear had been permanently
damaged.

"You seem anxious," the vestibular specialist observed,
somewhere off in the occluded sound and the darkness.

"I am."

She switched on the cold jets.

Mornings, we'd assemble with the other sufferers at the
hotel's front entryway, but far back enough that we didn't
trigger the automatic door. Only once the shuttle had arrived and its entry levered open did we scurry out of the
hotel, breathing little blades of air. Empty streets through
dirty windows. If my mother hadn't been beside me, I
wouldn't have known at first which stop was ours. We'd
double-check the schedule ("Gonda Building, Eighth
Floor, Desk 8 South: Clinical Neurophysiology"). The
packet would tell us how much time to expect and what
not to eat or drink, but it wouldn't describe the test in
any detail. Even so, the technicians sometimes appeared
surprised when I asked them what was going to happen.

"Now? Well, we're going to tape these coils on your
skin to test your autonomic reflexes."

"What will I experience? Just, you know, so I know."

"You'll feel a tingling on your skin. Some people think it feels like bugs under their skin."

Nervous about what the tests would reveal, nervous about the unknown, I'd recite all the Yeats I could in my head as procedures commenced: *Hands, do what you're bid / Bring the balloon of the mind* . . . I'm seated in a closet-sized apparatus that jerks and spins in the dark while lasers track the movements of my eyes: *And I will have some peace when I am there / For peace comes dropping slow* . . . I click the button when I hear a noise: *She bid me take life easy, as the grass grows on the weirs* . . .

On the last day, late in the afternoon, I sat in the office of the final specialist I'd meet on my visit, awaiting her appraisal. She arrived with a neutral expression, all business.

"Basically," she said, "your ears are probably deformed. We can't see them so we can't know exactly how."

"I see," I answered, watching my mother tense. She'd traveled a thousand miles. "Can you be more specific at all? And about why this only started a few years back?"

"Yes," she said, "It's called Ménière's disease—" she began to explain the characteristics of the average case, but I stopped her.

"Sorry—I know we have limited time. Did you have a look at the notes I sent ahead? About the unusual aspects of my case? The way sound comes and goes, or why I need to use this cane?"

"I've read the notes the other doctors here compiled for me." She was typing. This was going to be difficult.

"So you didn't see my hearing chart over time."

"I saw the test you took here. It shows damage."

"Right, but it comes and goes. That's unusual. I'd like to account for that and, if possible, to see if I can make it come and go a little less. Or reduce the tinnitus or—"

"What I see here is damage," she replied, growing steely. This had become a confrontation. I was a problem now, someone to be pacified and dispatched.

I produced the copy of the hearing tests I carry with me and scooted it onto her desk: "Look at those numbers rise and fall and rise and fall. Really, look here—have you ever seen that happen?"

She puffed up. My attitude was not good. "Your ears," she said, making her eyes wide, "are really screwed up, okay? And we're not going to know why until you're dead and we cut you open."

I didn't want to look at my mother.

"Can you read through the notes now, please?"

She didn't have the time. I could make an appointment if I liked "with a specialist."

I felt the room spin.

"Wait, so you're not a specialist?"

"I'm an ENT. But you need to speak to an otologist. Or a neurotologist. They're booked and can't see you today."

"But we *can't* come back. I don't have any money and my mother"—I looked at her when I gestured and saw she was aghast—"paid for my travel here. My card is nearly maxed out with medical debt. We *can't* do this again." This doctor was on the defensive now, which didn't help me, but I wanted her sympathy, for my mother if not for me.

I hadn't gone about it properly from the start, though, and she'd had enough. "I can't handle money stuff." She waved her hands. "I can't have a conversation about money. I'm giving you my recommendation, but I will not discuss money."

Why had I dragged my poor mother here?

"I'll wait," I decided, and said aloud, only half-aware of what noise my mouth would make next, "right here for an otologist."

She said, "You don't intimidate me. I am trying to help."

It's wrong of me to judge her. She had a schedule but, unlike most doctors, she had no financial incentive to hie me along. Mayo physicians don't earn more the more patients they see—in fact Mayo was the first clinic in the world to put its doctors on salary—but she had to get me out of her office because I was demanding she give me answers she simply didn't have. No one, it turns out, had those answers. And because she was a graduate of medical school, she was duty bound to bluster and present herself, when cornered, as stony. Quite a few specialists seem to feel they must behave this way.

Exasperated, she led me to the office of an audiologist. I was pleased. By now, most of the audiologists I'd met struck me as every bit as intelligent as most doctors, but there was a difference. Doctors tend to have far more stamina than most people: they need to, merely to survive the intensively competitive environment at medical school and the grueling thirty-hour shifts of resident training. Because they're possessed of such stamina, they tend to assume that everyone else is too; an unhappy side effect of this can be a brusque manner with their patients. Why is this guy sitting there whining about a little ringing in his ears? Nothing compared to a day and a half in the ER during a pileup.

This particular audiologist was thin and bald, with the passionate but otherworldly eyes of a mad scientist. I immediately felt confident he would diagnose me.

"Sit and face me." He took my chin in his hand and, without warning, jerked my head to the right. And again. Now the left.

"Ha!" he said. "I just caught something there that the test missed. All right, now I'm going to ask you a series of yes or no questions. Do you get dizzy in malls, supermarkets, places like that?"

I was dizzy everywhere, so I said yes.

"Do you get dizzy when something moves?"

Of course.

"Mm-hmm. How about staring at a screen?"

After that went on for a bit he handed me a pamphlet and told me I had something introduced to the literature a few years prior, a condition known as chronic subjective dizziness. "It's treated with antidepressants but—since it isn't entirely inside your head—we also use physical therapy."

He recommended a specific physical therapist ("Oh, you're lucky she's in Denver"). When I managed to score an appointment later that month, she laid me flat on a table and set weights on my pelvis and legs. Then she activated a spinning tube that resembled a lampshade with lozenges cut from its surface; this projected a series of whirling lights against the wall. The idea was to provoke dizziness. It worked.

"Eventually," she said, "after a number of weeks, this won't make you dizzy anymore, or it shouldn't, if Mayo Clinic is correct."

Several months later, no less dizzy than I'd arrived, we parted ways. But first, she leveled with me. "Mayo Clinic," she said, "is going to tell you that you have chronic subjective dizziness because one of their doctors invented it."

We don't really know why people get CSD, my pamphlet reads, going on to ask, *How can I be sure that CSD is what I have?* Answer:

> Research studies show that if you fit the criteria for CSD described in the first section of this booklet and have had a complete evaluation, it is not likely that other diagnoses have been missed.

So, like Ménière's, chronic subjective dizziness is a diagnosis of exclusion, a lack of understanding made into a mouthful of air. We know that something is wrong, but not why; we know that some treatments might ameliorate things here and there, but only for some patients. And we talk like we've got that nailed.

"The thing about specialists," a friend in financial journalism ventured—I'd been ghostwriting for him to make a little cash—"is that even if they're only 80 percent sure what's wrong with you, they'll sound as though they're 100 percent sure, and they'll sound that way every time."

Another friend, a wise woman, tells me, "Specialists come down with MDiety, this supreme confidence that's so often a load of bull." The certainty with which the Mayo audiologist assured me I had CSD, and the satisfied smile with which he typed out his instructions felt as solid to me as a concrete floor. He also told me that in all probability I would lose my hearing in both ears and develop long-term balance problems, a condition called oscillopsia, a balance disorder common to those with late-stage Ménière's in both ears. The eyes, ears, and brain are three legs of a tripod maintaining balance. Just as vertigo attacks cause victims to lose control over the movements of their own eyes, so will the degenerative destruction of that system cause objects to blur and oscillate and bob up and down. Have you ever tried to film an object while walking toward it? Provided you aren't holding a Steadicam, the object bobs up and down far more than your visual field seemed to do: your brain could maintain a seemingly steady focus all the while, but your camera couldn't. That's what walking is like with oscillopsia: your eyes and sense of touch are all that's left to balance with. Without signals from your ear to guide you, you'll lurch or fall in a dark room, or a dim one, or one that seems, for whatever reason, to be in motion (say, because an object in the distance suddenly moves). Even in daylight, you'll have trouble walking straight.

It felt like a sentence. What had I done to deserve it?

. . .

"I just wonder," I said on the morning of the concluding visit with my original Mayo internist, "whether—even if 'Ménière's disease' ends up being as close as we can come to a diagnosis . . . I just wondered if maybe there was new research you could recommend I look through, or some trial drug, or some reason for a radical and a probably unsound hope? Even another Mayo doctor I could tele-conference with when I'm home?"

He shook his head. "What you hear from one doctor at Mayo you will hear from every doctor. Our instructions and our diagnoses are standardized throughout the enterprise."

"What about something like chronic Lyme? Should I investigate that?"

Again, he shook his head. "Our policy is that chronic Lyme does not exist."

"I see. I was just coming here for a fresh take on things. I thought with so many brilliant minds together . . . I thought they might see my case afresh, maybe save some hearing before it disappears."

He said, "The place you have come to is one of the most conservative institutions in the world."

Mayo's emphasis for most visits, Seltman and Berry tell us, is less concerned with research than with standardiza-tion, though they quote Stephen Swensen, Mayo's director of quality, as saying "a standard treatment protocol is an incendiary concept for many doctors—they call it 'cook-book medicine.'" Swensen goes on to explain that this is what's best for the patient, that care should be the same "no matter what door they open." Perhaps he is right.

Waiting at the front door of the clinic for the shuttle to ferry us one last time to our hotel, I was at a loss for what to say. I felt a sensation in my stomach I've only known a few times in my life: the sense I'd been dropped off at a new elementary school where I had no friends. I felt entirely bereft.

"I used to think they were such a big deal," Mom said. "I mean look at this, this whole building, all this art. Now, let's just say I am *very* disappointed. I think they may just be making money. The whole thing."

I don't agree with her. I know the doctors we saw all did their best. To the best of their knowledge I would gradually lose the rest of my hearing and balance, probably in a matter of years. To the best of their knowledge, any additional dizziness was caused by a condition, CSD, the existence of which I could not find one non-Mayo doctor to affirm. (No psychiatrist I could find in Denver had heard of the condition, and all discarded the pamphlets I provided them with "Well, let's just work together and see where we go.") About the roaring in my ears and the hearing loss, Mayo can do nothing because no one can.

I wasn't feeling any better about things when my mother and I went our separate ways at the Minneapolis airport, she back east where I grew up, and me to Denver where I'd try to come to terms with what was happening. I know she felt as blue as I felt, but she kept her head up and managed a smile. I wondered how long I'd be able to recognize her voice on the phone.

As I walked to my connecting gate—I had time to kill before it boarded—I glanced at some of the airport

TVs, each tuned to CNN. The video making the rounds that week online had finally found its way to 24/7 news, anything to fill the time. It showed a soldier coming home from war—which war wasn't clear—and being tearfully reunited with his dog. It was touching, as all of those videos are, but as I gave in to the tears it provoked, as intended, I began to distrust it. Or, rather, I began to wonder what it was obscuring, what other truth this happier truth papered over.

Any number of soldiers don't ever come home from those impossible wars. Any number of families futilely fantasize about such a scene. But no video of the carnage our explosives and our bullets have caused throughout the Middle East will win as many clicks, or break as many American hearts.

So it is with our diseases and our cures. Around the time I first fell ill, another viral video made the rounds, this one of a woman getting her cochlear implant switched on for the first time. She was young, thin, tattooed. She was vulnerable—you could identify. She'd been deaf since birth. The machines activated. Immediately, she started weeping.

Cochlear implants can be a wonder for the profoundly deaf, but they aren't anything like natural hearing and they don't work for everyone. There are as many stories of shock and disappointment at their first activation as there are of awe. These videos don't go viral.

Before I became unwell I thought, like a lot of us do, that doctors had bags full of magic. I thought that if they couldn't fix what was wrong, at least they could find

a way to make you feel somewhat better. But there are
thousands of diseases we have not yet cured and thousands of those that don't yet have their March of Dimes,
their Betty Ford.

I didn't leave Mayo Clinic with either a cure or a reliable prognosis, but I did leave wiser than I'd come. Delays
due to extremes of cold had somehow bumped me into
business class—a piece of luck that wasn't lost on me. Ice
cream was served in stemless wineglasses. Wine was free.
I ordered a red and watched the white prairie gradually
attain the bronze of a desert. I took in all that I could see.

No Satori

The night before Viv's funeral, my right ear emptied of the roar. It had been a year since the ear registered external sound. As that Yale specialist had told me, "When the ear's been unresponsive for more than three months, the rule is to say it's gone." The left ear, meanwhile, had been working on and off for weeks.

Now it was back, but who knew for how long. I ran my finger up the pinna—the bit that resembles a shell. Only treble, but it conducted. How much?

I knew exactly how to proceed. Carefully, I laid myself down on my childhood bed—mattress from 1978, sheets from 1986—and set in place an expensive pair of Audio Technica headphones I'd been saving against the day. Jascha Heifetz, back in 1952, in Hollywood, playing Bach's Partitas for solo violin. It's vertiginous, sinister, and somehow a kind of duet, the way he plays it, a dance at the edge of a cliff.

"That's the wonderful thing about Bach," an old writer once told me when I said I'd gotten into the habit of waking up to the Partitas. "He heals you."

"The thing you have to remember about Heifetz's playing," said a camera repairman I used to drink gin with, "is that he wasn't adding passion that wasn't there. The passion was there already—Bach is incredibly passionate. Heifetz just isn't a prude."

Music fixes nothing but mood, but mood can be everything. For the last three days I'd been listless and defeated. Only now that I'd gotten my right ear back did I feel to myself as though my thoughts made any sense.

In the week that followed, traveling the familiar wooded streets of Norwich, every memory rode on a measure of sound. How could I question the way music or language or ambient noise tied in to everything I'd ever seen or felt or tasted? I remembered a story Viv told me. She was talking about her husband, my grandfather, ten years after he died. This specific part of the story was an apology for why she missed him. It wasn't necessary, of course. I missed him too.

"He used to say things that made me laugh. I don't know—we'd be walking across ice one day in high school and he'd say, *It sounds like Jack eating celery.* Jack was his father. I can't explain, but I still think about that when I cross over ice. Jack eating celery. He always said things like that. I thought they were funny."

Now in my old bed, in the house where I grew up, I took in the room. The carpet at night in the weak light of a lamp down the hall was dark blue, almost black; the walls were robin's egg. There was paper on one wall with red, dark blue, and yellow splatters. I didn't know it so well anymore that I didn't see it. I saw it that night.

My sister's room, from the brain of the same designer in '87, was going to be pink. She pushed to make it green. I never thought to push.

Against the floor, along the wall, reposed a neon-blue phone with a spiral cord. This antique thing was where a lot of my life was lived at age fourteen. With Cathy mostly. She sat behind me in homeroom and we talked for an average of an hour each night from our first to our third year of high school. I'd finish whatever shouting match I was holding with my father and then, when the house fell quiet, I'd pour out my restlessness onto Cathy, equally restless three towns away.

The last time I saw her I said, "We burned so many hours that I wish I remembered what we talked about."

She said, "I remember it really well."

Cathy came through Denver shortly before Viv died. She'd flown in from Strasbourg for a conference. Could we get an early dinner?

Eating at restaurants with a single person was still possible then, but under anything short of ideal conditions eating with more than two or three was nearly hopeless. Not because I couldn't hear the other end of the table (no one could) but because of the way whoever talked at me— the lips I needed to look at—dodged away to catch this or that someone else was saying. Conversation has a pattern on such occasions, like wind moving shadows in tall grass. There are no straight lines. Conversations bubble and then separate into two or three. They ricochet, contact, and collide like a billiards break. The collective ethology of a flock of birds is what I think about when everyone's talking in groups of one or two and suddenly the whole table laughs. Not knowing what they're laughing about, I pretend to laugh half with them and half to myself, or at myself.

Cathy and I would be eating alone. I was already having trouble on the phone last time we talked, though that isn't why we fell out of touch. And for chance reasons—or for deterministic reasons no one understands—my hearing wasn't any good on the evening she was free, so I suggested a place with tables outdoors on a quiet street.

The sky was overcast. She shivered in her jacket. Then she said what I heard as, "[   ]"

"Hmm? Sorry I couldn't catch that"

"I said I have a *challenging time* in Strasbourg. The French [   ] but they always [   ]."

"Oh?"

"There's no word for [   ]."

"How so?"

"[   ] try to explain the idea of *kindness* to Philippe but even though he's [   ], and he doesn't [   ]."

Knowing Cathy, and the sort of thing that might bother her, I made an educated guess. "So if they have no word for . . . 'kindness' is what you said? Do you mean they don't *act* kind either, like they don't understand the concept?"

She nodded.

"Then how do they describe what Jesus was like?"

"Nice, cool."

"They don't emulate him?"

"Oh no! Ha ha! No, they [   ] weakness."

The window to the inside of the restaurant was open beside our table and I could feel noise rolling out of it.

Cathy spoke and gestured toward it.

I said, "Yeah, let's try to close it. Is it loud?"

She looked at me confusedly and shouted, as I leaned close to her, "Yeah! It's just people shouting at each other! It's really loud!"

Eventually, having avoided the obvious subject for a polite length of time, Cathy asked what she had to ask.

"So what [   ]?" She pointed at her ears.

I talked through the seven-minute version, which was about as short as I could shave it and still anticipate the usual follow-ups. The list goes dizziness, variable hearing, vertigo, roaring. Yes, the kind when the whole room spins. Hours. No, believe it or not, it's the hearing bit that's worse—harder to connect with the world. No, doctors don't understand this stuff. Yes, I've been everywhere. No, we don't know if I'll lose all of it, but the odds are good. No, we don't know—it could happen tomorrow.

"[   ]."

"I know," I could guess at what she'd just said, "I know."

"[   ] Elisa?"

"Elisa's been wonderful," I said. "I'm the one who's been difficult."

When our server appeared, Cathy asked if she could help us close the window beside us when she wound her way back indoors—someone was needed both inside and outside to accomplish this.

"That's great." Cathy said once we'd all worked to wedge the old thing shut. "Now I can stop shouting all the time. [   ]?"

Last April, in Connecticut. I sat with Viv in her unsteady folding chairs and watched the wildlife in the yard and the trees. For fifty years, she and Art lived in the Victorian on Washington Street; for the last ten it's been only her. A dozen generations of thrushes and flycatchers and raccoons made steady lives in the old barn and the wetlands at the foot of the hill.

Three centuries ago the wetland behind the house was a riverbed, but the waters were diverted and the muddy bed filled on its own with sedge and long grass. Past the meadow and the copse of cedar hides the cemetery where we keep the bones of our local *Declaration of Independence* signer, a dull man from town, and also of Benedict Arnold's mother, Hannah. Her modest stone is vandalized from time to time and patched less expertly as the years persist.

"I suppose you'll be going home soon," Viv said. I was having a good day and could hear her well enough. At ninety-eight, always, even on my bad days, she remembered to speak up for me.

"I'll be back in June." After I'd taught a class in Denver, one whose major goal was to pay for the tickets back and forth. I missed New England.

"Well, look, there's something I want you to do for me before you go. I want you to go into that attic and, well first I want you to put peppermint down to keep the bats away—just sprinkle it everywhere—and then I want you to carry down that trunk by the stairs. I want to see what's in it."

Back in the living room, windows shut against a breeze, we pulled handfuls of old snapshots and decomposing albums from the trunk in a wash of mildew. The corners of the windows were stained glass and thin curtains blocked the edges below them so the only light was the same amber and mauve as the tinted glass.

She handed me a snapshot of Art beside a grapefruit-sized ball with six antennas, like a daddy longlegs in rictus.

"That's Sputnik." She pronounced the u to rhyme with you. She might have been right—I don't know Russian—but her Jackie-comes-to-southeastern-Connecticut accent wasn't free of foibles: Hershey was *Hurzy*, Jay Leno was *Jay Lean-o*.

The couch sagged underneath us and I let my muscles go, at ease in a room where I'd spent so many afternoons. But there on these little cards was evidence of a prehistory that had nothing to do with this room or with me or even Viv. Upright men in mustaches froze themselves in studios, swells in applejack hats leaned on stone walls in gaggles, their arms around grinning girls.

Viv sighed beside me. Beach house sold, those were her summers: bright outdoors full of alien life and closed dark spaces with her thoughts.

Wrong to call the little one in my hand black and white: it was faded ochre, beige, gold. A vanishing man in a white mustache and an oversize '20s overcoat stands beneath a bower of twigs (his stride has been arrested but he doesn't mind) while a pool of overexposure creates a knot of light below his waist that threatens to pull him down into it.

Viv no sooner got a glimpse of it before she moved to take it. I wouldn't get it back.

"Oh but this . . ."

I'd never seen her cry before, never really seen her sad.

". . . oh, dear, he was my *love* . . ."

Italics are cheap. *Love* wasn't strident, but everything went into it.

"He was my friend," she said, and was quiet for a half minute. I looked at the photographer's shadow, intrusive in the blur: his arms were down at his chest, dating the shot from when the camera's sight was located on top of the box. Had they used mirrors?

"He always came into a room and . . ." She took a minute. "He would stamp his feet one after the other to hello the house. He was so fun."

Fun she said like *love*.

She blotted her eyes but she didn't put the picture back on the pile.

She was his granddaughter. It had been, she explained to me, eighty years since she'd looked at his face in life.

I thought about, but I didn't talk about, how every year until her balance went in her midseventies, she'd wait half a second after she walked into my parents' house, and then she'd stomp her feet one after the other against the floor.

So I knew more, and I smiled at her a little more bravely than usual when I left in the late afternoon. I never saw her again.

Back in Denver weeks later, outdoors at a bar for older, settled hipsters, the hearing in my left ear quivered off and on, absent then present. I'd been sipping club soda. I ordered another.

A group of us had been talking about smoking since a woman three tables over did a very odd thing and lit a cigarette in a public place. Elisa said, "I've never smoked— and I still don't want to start—but I've changed my thinking about it. I used to think it was stupid to smoke, but I just turned that corner where I'm closer to seventy than zero all of a sudden, and so I feel like I do understand what people mean when they say, 'Well, something's going to kill you anyway' . . . I mean I'm not going to *do* it, but it doesn't seem as stupid as it used to seem."

"Well," I said, "you don't just drop dead from it. I mean, you suffer."

"Everyone suffers!"

We were drinking with Aaron, who jumped in with, "Life is always getting shorter."

Random acts of self-pity had always been an arrow in my quiver. I carefully extracted one and set it.

"Well, that's one of the things that bums me out about losing my hearing so quickly in my thirties. That's just goodbye forever to certain ideas, certain things. I mean, I was probably never going to hear a live performance of the Ring Cycle, but now I know for *sure* I never will. So that wonderful poignancy of possibility is lost to me; I can't cushion my head on the fantasy, or the maybe. The great maybe."

Indulgent, they often let me speak at length like this, but this time Elisa responded with, "But there's another way to see it. That you . . ."

"That he never has to sit through the Ring Cycle?" Aaron offered. I laughed at this.

"Well yes, that, but also that you can devote the time you would have spent sitting there to something else. It can sharpen your focus."

We talked about this for a while, deciding I should spend more time looking at art, now that I was less able to listen to it. I could walk without a cane the next day so Elisa and I hoofed it together to the Kirkland Museum. We hadn't seen it since we moved to Denver, so why not? It was filled with deco sofas when we got there, and leather straps on the ceiling where Vance Kirkland suspended himself facedown to paint the cheesy swirls of his celestial visions onto wall-sized canvas. The director caught me making some notes beside one of the more trancy pictures, a glowing orange Venusberg.

"That's one of his '70s things—did you see the straps? Come up to my office and I'll show you some more."

We advanced upstairs to a dignified room packed with paintings where he moved straight to the stereo and twisted the volume knob on the background Holst until it blocked from me anything he might say.

"Is this ... this picture a Beddows," I asked, "or ... ?"

"[   ]."

I gave him my all-occasions smile, a sort of hapless half shrug.

"[   ], or if you'd rather, [   ]?

"Oh I see. Sure?"

"[   ]."

"Come again?"

"I said it was my *mother too,* back then."

Still shaking my head about how tricky that was, and how ignobly I sulked out of that office, I exited the gift shop into the Denver sun. That's when Elisa and I were nearly killed.

I probably exaggerate. The kid was just trying to scare us, but it worked well enough that I was still shaking two hours later. He roared his Chevy truck through the alley that ran between Pearl and Washington just as we crossed in front of it and he didn't stop, in fact he revved the truck even faster. We scattered out of his way less than a second before he would have struck us both and sent us into the street, broken bones at best. As he turned right and sped, he laughed loud, not a real laugh but a stagey taunt.

I didn't get much of a look at him: maybe eighteen to twenty-two, a white kid, browned from the sun. Driving a car around pedestrians gave him a sense of power and he clearly found it entertaining. Little sociopath fuck. Fuck him, fuck *him*.

On adrenaline, I took off running after the truck when it stopped at the light on Washington. What did I want to do? Murder him, pull open his door, beat him in the street.

The light turned.

In the quiet house, sky going blue, I felt a throb in my right ear like a jet taking off. A dull hum filled my left. Gradually, the dull hum rose, like some experiment in early electronic music, something for a Theremin and ham radio. By 9 p.m., the roar was all I could find room for, so I decided it was time to meditate. Health professionals, friends, various books all recommended this course, and I'd been trying. I set up a cushion in the study and shut the door. No street noise, no hum from the refrigerator, no late calls of flying birds. As I looked ahead and attempted to clear my mind, I was called back at every second into the noise. If anything, meditating made it louder, the hum now coming like a siren. My teeth clenched. I tried to touch it away with the word *thinking*. But of course I wasn't thinking, I was listening.

When I used to meditate years ago I'd happily anticipate that moment when the clutter in my mind got swept away. I'd relish the little noises that appeared when I could finally settle into them: the breathing of the hall, water pipes, the master's shuffle behind us. I attained no satori in those days but I did find I could think of nothing and that it brought me back, showed me where I was.

Now I noticed myself grinding my teeth. I'd been in my head, escaping the noise. But it's a mistake to try to find the other side of it. Instead I was intended to . . . to what? Hear it but not feel it. Or feel it and let it go?

So as the hour waxed I dove in again, kept my teeth apart, kept my breath consistent, if inaudible. Then the roar became something else. Don't think about what to call it. Listen.

"I'll be just fine," I told Elisa on her way out of the apartment, "you just go and have a good time."

She left for a party. I went for a walk. Big sun and small rain like every day that summer. The sky had cleared only a minute before so I decided to walk for a bit and then sit outside and read. I would have rather gone to the party with Elisa, but I'd only been able to hear one voice at a time in quiet rooms that week—I knew I'd just feel more alone there.

I ordered a mint tea in the quiet shop down the street and took a table. Suddenly, I became aware of my hearing dropping even farther away. The roaring in both ears grew louder, yes, but more telling was that the conversation at the table beside me—which I could never hear clearly—had dropped off entirely. Mouths moved around me but no sound escaped. I clicked my wooden pencil against the metal table. Nothing.

I fished the tiny remote from my hip pocket and clicked the volume up. No, just the roar. I cleared my own throat to try to hear it sound. Blank. I clicked it up more. Nothing. More. I could hear something faintly now—you know how voices sound when you're far-off and you can hear that they're coming, but not the words they carry? That's how my own voice came to my ears. I maxed the remote, knowing the distortion at this volume would obliterate any sense of human speech.

What surprised me was that it wasn't just the human speech that blurred and fell apart but every report around me: a cup on a saucer, a barking dog, or a laugh from two tables off all asserted themselves with the same electronic *pock*.

The chances, I said to myself, that this roar would last longer than a single day or two were low. It had been over a year since something like that made me panic. But I couldn't help but feel lonely. I'd been looking forward to an evening with a book at the coffee shop, and now what I wanted more than anything was a human voice. The phone became inutile, even with the headset. I wouldn't be able to understand anyone if I drove to the party, I'd end up making a spectacle of myself. People only tolerate so much of that.

It was when I arrived home, and only after the door shut behind me, that I gave in to panic. The vertigo began in earnest, my legs going out from under me and my cheek hitting the floor. It's more accurate to say the floor circled up toward me, followed by the ceiling it merged against, hovered with. It caught me inside itself, the spin, clutching on to the underside of a sliding closet door as though it was my mother's hand. If I kept gripping it like that I'd unsettle it from its hinges. I knew this but I couldn't stop. I couldn't stop spinning or holding on. I whimpered like a kid. I couldn't move.

The attic of Viv's now-empty house. Murk clung to the rafters but a few slivers of white light came through the low windows at the gables, making it enchanting rather than darkly mysterious. Every time I walked down to the second floor with a box of ancient records and stacked it against the wall to Viv's room (there was a tiny window with no shade opening from her room to the hall—why?), I marveled at how small the place had become in the week I'd spent cleaning it out, the mystery vanishing. Ten years ago or more, she and Art let me house a bunch of wedding guests here; we told ghost stories in the attic until Shafer, a burly redheaded Texan, said, "Can we please get out of here, *please?*"

A cardboard box full of 45s filled my arms, a bunch of old blues records. How would I get them back to Denver? With what spare cash? They'd remain. They'd be thrown away.

Outdoors, where the greensward dips to the stone wall and the wetland, on what used to be the banks of a tributary of the Yantic River, I set up one of Viv's ancient card tables. This one had lived in the upstairs kitchen, unused since the '60s when Viv and Art paid off the mortgage and quit renting out the upper floor. Around it I positioned two of the wooden-slat folding chairs that had always sat outside in summer; they were an ancient, powdery mauve that came off on my hands even when I was a child. That done, I reached for my backpack and extracted from it a bottle of Viognier and two twelve-inch grinder sandwiches from Irene's, the former Pizza Kitchen, a place whose counter I've stood at waiting for takeout since before I could make memories. I set the steak-and-cheese on the side facing away from the big old white barn and the BLT (fist-sized tangles of bacon, iceberg flakes, some rumors of white tomato) on my own side of the table.

In a few minutes Golaski was there, tearing a corner off the steak-and-cheese grinder with his teeth in that ultracivilized style he has wherein he can finish a big sandwich before I've started on my second half but I'm not sure I've ever once seen him lower his head or chew.

I apologized for the spot, although I didn't have to. "I think I got attached not just because of Viv, but because this place was my last connection to this dream of shabby gentility I've always had. You know, the guy in the frayed sweater who's got stacks of dough in the bank."

"Is there any way . . . ?" He wiped at the corners of his mouth with a nonabsorbent grinder shop napkin but there was nothing there. Golaski played shabby genteel better than I ever could: old sweaters, loafers. He'd been teaching in Connecticut this morning and the next day he'd teach at Brown, though both jobs were contingent; he worried about them. "I just wonder if there was some way you could convince your parents to hold off selling so that you and Elisa could move in and live for a few years and fix the place up . . ."

"Oh, we're past that. I get you, but we're past it. I mean that ship has sailed. Dad's been using his credit cards as a paycheck for a decade. Maybe more. They need to sell it."

"It's just a shame because I know you and she had a real attachment. Just the last time I was here, when we were walking through that graveyard, you were telling me about how she was ninety-eight and she'd told you a joke—and it was a good one!"

He was indulging me. That was all right. It had been a good joke.

This fat woman gets stuck on the toilet. Her husband says, "I'll call the plumber." He gives her his derby hat to put over her lap, for modesty. The plumber arrives and says, "I can get her unstuck, my friend, but the guy in the derby hat is a goner."

Golaski said, "You know, I hate to say it, but do you know what would be perfect?"

"Another bottle of wine?"

He sat back, emphatic "*Yes.*"

"We'll walk through the meadow. There's a place on the other side." I hadn't walked through the meadow since 1994. I figured it as a blizzard of Lyme ticks, but I led him down the tree-shaded slate streets two houses to the north and through an archway, down the slab steps to a meadow clear out of a dream.

I had one good ear that afternoon, and it let me hear Golaski's voice. What I also heard: the brush of my feet in grass and dry leaves and the pops of breaking twigs.

Wind: the stop and start of it you can't predict, or control. Skittering insects, chirps of forty birds, fifty clicks, chitters, squees, throat clearing, a rusty hinge squeal, a piping, pinched flutes, calls like a finger on a wet glass, return calls. The green insect almost too small to see— you couldn't make out its shape, just a speck of green. A machine loud enough to sound close, but it carried so you couldn't be sure, maybe a mower.

"What on earth?" Golaski said. He swept his arms, theatrically indignant, but beneath that I could see he really was in awe. Awe was easy to feel.

"You *have* this in your back*yard*?"

"Once upon a time."

Everywhere the grass was green and high: dales spread with light-green hedges and big flat expanses of sea waves of long grass. At the end of it, just distinguishable in mild haze: Viv's white barn. I'd been up in the roof of it two months earlier, tweeting pictures of my face in a safety mask, fireplace shovel in my hand, scraping bat guano. I couldn't imagine a situation in which I'd stand in this meadow again.

"It's easy," I said, "you just walk through here ten minutes and you come out on Town Street and there's the liquor store, and there used to be a sheet music store there above it. My sister had to go there for dancing class."

"You and Elisa could have hosted poetry readings on the lawn," he said, while real butterflies beat their wings around us. "I'm sorry about that. What if you offered to pay rent?"

"No, the house is gone and I'm going deaf. I just feel like, I don't know, like my narrative is just loss lately."

Golaski said something I wasn't hearing, and I registered the click down in my ability to take in sound along with the soft of the meadow and the stone bench with the small-town graffiti beside us ("MEGIE & HOW") and the high-summer green of the circling trees and hedges.

In Denver, I wake up while the dark drains out of the sky and I can hear the birds again. The calls wake me. It's been weeks since I heard the birds in Connecticut, so these noises stagger when they filter in, pull me out of an anxious dream.

Elisa's awake too and she isn't groggy. She takes as a given that they're there.

I say, "There's one of them, the angry one who's fainter than the starling."

"He's farther away," she says. Of course.

"All right, it may be starting to disappear again now," I tell her. She takes hold of my arm and rubs it with slow strokes while I listen to the birds fade. Then she nuzzles against me and she's asleep again, a gentle weight on my chest.

I can hear them fading, going—they'll be gone at any second. As I listen to the last catches of song, I can feel my heart break in every sound. Don't let that one be the last one. Don't let that one. Don't let that.

Intermezzo

Coolness—
the sound of the bell
    as it leaves the bell.

—YOSA BUSON, *trans.* ROBERT HASS

Four Music Lessons

The unreachable green on both sides of Lawler Lane flashed by the windows of Dad's MG as he tapped the wheel in time. "Galveston" played, Glen Campbell's version. It started with a gallop—I imagined horses breaking free—flush of orchestra. I knew even at nine what victory sounds like.

"Galveston," Campbell sings, "Oh, Galveston! I still hear your sea winds blowin' . . ." There's a big-eyed girl and he's not with her. Why? "She was twenty-one when I left Galveston." The music feels rushed and wrong.

Then cannons flash, or we're told they flash, and before we can make any sense of it, "I am so afraid of dying." Songs never talk about dying. Dad doesn't listen to stuff like that. He wouldn't say something like that.

Dad focused on his day in the morning; we didn't talk much as we drove. His name had been cropping up in the local paper and he never seemed happy to see it. He was angry at home. I looked for the kind of clues a nine-year-old looks for and I wasn't sure what I saw.

The Glen Campbell tape rolled in his tape deck all that year, and some of it made sense to me. "Wichita Lineman" I understood—it was about a lonely man and it sounded lonely. But it didn't make Dad especially quiet, or whatever he was feeling as he fixed his eyes ahead and fell into himself.

"I clean my gun, and dream of Galveston." It's the cleaning, the readiness for violence, that felt eeriest. I knew there was violence in my dad and this sad song evoked it. He didn't become angry in the car, but the song warned me not to talk. How? There wasn't any anger in the music. Eventually I decided the story could only be about Vietnam.

Vietnam alone evoked that look on Dad's face when it came up: a pained triumph that didn't rule out the threat of violence. I'd already learned this at home. To understand it better, I picked "Why Did We Lose the Vietnam War?" from a list of possible subjects for history reports. I asked Dad where I should start researching. He said, "Give it here," and filled three pages in my notebook—a history that painted the French as the original cold warriors. "Having researched this subject thoroughly," it concluded, "it is not at all clear to me that we 'lost' the Vietnam War."

He slid it across the table. "There you go, boy—all set."

I didn't question Dad, just took the notebook. And I didn't open my mouth while Galveston played. I listened. The trees flashed.

I spent the summer of 1995 shoveling hot patch into asphalt craters in my hometown, and that's where I met Stan. Mustachioed, solitary, Stan seemed too young to have wrung though two marriages and an LSD habit so bad that it turned him to fanatical religion. I didn't think he could be over thirty-five. That summer in Stan's Public Works truck, I grew repeatedly amazed by how much of the early 1960s seemed alive in the men I worked alongside, though they must have only been children then.

"It ain't the '60s no more, Telgarsky," they'd warn each other. Even Stan got a dose.

"Poor Stan," said an old guy I drove out to the quarry with one afternoon to have fresh patch poured into the truck bed. "He still thinks it's the '60s, but it ain't the '60s no more."

While other trucks played the Beatles and the Rolling Stones, Stan's was purely blues.

"It ain't the '60s no more, Stan," Pete shouted as his own truck turned down Laurel Hill. Stan wanted to take a break away from Pete—which, if you knew Pete, made sense—finally shutting the engine down three streets away so we could stare at the leaves and listen to the blues. It sounded like John Lee Hooker but without Hooker's voice.

He told me a part of his story, organized as a recovery narrative. We'd been comparing drug stories for most of that ride, but Stan had me whipped. It took place in the last moments of his wild years, after he'd been rolling on LSD for the third day straight. His daughter was young then, barely two, and the day was hot. "My hands were sweating, but I only noticed that when I picked her up. And as I was holding her there I remembered that sweat can transfer all those chemicals. Like, just by holding my daughter, just by doing that, I could be getting her high. I was all done at that point. No more drugs, and nothing that made me crazy for drugs neither."

He told me about his church, a charismatic minister with a bunch of folding chairs in a basement. "We just groove in there, you know." He said the word "groove" like he was grooving on it.

"It ain't the *music* the devil loves, it's the lyrics."

"So the lyrics have to be religious?"

"Yeah, but not just the words." Grade-two hot patch cooled in the back of the truck, which would make it harder to shovel later on. "It's the spirit they're sung in. They've gotta come from the right place. But music is just music—ain't ever bad on its own."

I had a cassette tape of Paganini's *Caprices* I'd borrowed from the library, and I slid it into the tape deck one evening as we pulled our gloves off and started the long drive back to the depot.

Niccolò Paganini, I'd learned only the week before, was a contemporary of Lord Byron's who, like Byron, encouraged rumors that his talent was born of a pact with the devil. But Stan said God loved all music that didn't have lyrics. We listened to the first caprice as we set off for a spot where it would be safe to dump the rest of the hot patch, now too cold to use. I'd heard the tape just once before and smiled to remember how with the very first notes, Paganini made the atmosphere haywire, a slippery violin that squeaks away from the player.

"No way, man," Stan said. Shaking his head, bothered for Paganini's sake. "That guy's way too nervous. That guy's living the wrong life."

Without the lights, all we could make out were the glow strips Namrata had the good sense to lay down in the wings. Golaski, dressed in black, waited beside me. The blackness of the drapes, floor, and the sliver of stage otherwise invisible from the wings made it impossible to take in one another clearly, impossible to see anything more than the deep-sea phosphorescence of those arrows.

I'd been asked to direct a play produced by the Harvard South Asian Association. There'd been Bollywood music playing and a din from the gathering crowd, so the sudden silence when the lights went down felt physical: there was no division now between the invisibility of the stage and my own vanishing.

Weeks ago, we'd decided to open the play with the sound of a Muslim call to prayer. There was no muezzin in the cast or crew, and only one volunteer seemed to have the whole of adhan in his head. I had my doubts when he first cleared his throat at rehearsal. Gokul didn't seem musical. He carried himself stiffly and majored, I think, in math. But of course I was wrong, and as the first *Allahu akbar* emerged I began to feel a little of what might entice a listener to turn to it. And then the Shahada: *Ashhadu alla ilaha illa Allah*. I furrowed my forehead with pleasure.

When I say I vanished in the darkness backstage, I mean for a play to work, a director's effort must appear invisible: the pieces I've put in place have to operate on their own. Considered that way, casting myself in a non-speaking role was little more than a way of gawking at the action from center stage, even taking an early bow. It was the last play I'd direct before I started going deaf, but I didn't know that then.

In my mind, in the dark, I reviewed what would happen next: Golaski and I would proceed onstage after Gokul's song, thick wooden dowels in our hands. The production called for two guards, and I wanted those guards to be alien. "Let the two *gora* do it," I told Aditi, using the South Asian slang for *white guy*, a word I'd only learned when I started directing Desi theater. Golaski and I were both the color of milk. I liked the switch.

But we couldn't come onstage quite yet. First, the silence had to lean into itself. Later, Golaski told me it wasn't as quiet as I'd remembered it. Apparently, I was whispering to myself under my breath. I asked him what he heard.

He said he'd only remembered one line, which I'd turned to say to him directly. Just as the first silence fell, I'd said, "*This is my favorite part.*"

Without music for most of two years, I've found that on good days, with the help of high-powered headphones, I can hear it still. Depending on the recording, the instrumentation, the pitch, it sometimes sounds the way it did, or close enough. Flutes are gone, and soft voices, and most of a piano too (not the *forte* part, but the *piano* part). Violins remain, and brass.

At first, I wanted only to hear my favorites, but now I want to fall in love again. I'd never given Bach's Orchestral Suites any attention so I'm trying them. Of course, I'd heard some in the past—you can't be alive and miss Bach's Air on a G string, the second movement of Suite no. 3. Any time is a good time to play it.

I play it today on Mediterranean Lane as I walk around blind curves, over the stone heaps of ruined walls, past towering, weatherworn barns. Orchestral suites are collections of dances, and I find myself surprised, pausing to admire guttered rivulets and overgrown fields that

144

used to be farms before the farmers fled west, by how much I want to move, puff my chest, strike out with my arms. The song is a dance.

I'm surprised, too, by how easily the sounds in my ears seem to command the things around me—the chipmunks dashing over the road, the lightly swaying elms—it all seems *orchestrated*.

Now, near-deaf but reprieved, I move with new pleasure. The final movement of Suite no. 3 is a dance, a gigue, pronounced like a Frenchman was attempting to say *jig*, because it is a jig: a prancing march, echoed at intervals by a wall of brass that leaps from nowhere.

Suddenly the street is playful, the houses are playful and the yards. A pair of deer stand motionless in a field. No: only one is real. The other is a deer statue that someone has put on their lawn.

The brass clears its throat to speak, then retreats, nears to speak.

The real deer bounds away. Then the statue bounds away.

II

Jack of die
you can hear the diamonds.

If I keep hearing them
I can be dead, just listening.

Because what I love is this song.

Would you die for it? I may. But chance
is involved here. I have a slightly better than fifty
percent chance of getting better. For a while at
least. They've done the statistics.
    I am no one, the new species, just like you.

—ALICE NOTLEY, *IN THE PINES*

The Trauma Test

Albert Camus called the feeling of the absurd—the feeling, for example, that my ears might be dying for no real reason; that I didn't *cause* this, or that few of us *cause* all the misfortune that befalls us, or particularly deserve it (nor would we particularly deserve reprieve; we don't *deserve* each morning's sunrise) a sensation of "sin without God." In Camus's metaphysics, the only thing to do in the face of the absurd is to revolt: to look the absurd in the eye and to carry on, to insure the absurd does not break you.

How could I look the absurd in the eye? I had one idea. Lighthouse was sending teachers to a homeless shelter in eastern Colorado as part of a community engagement program. A new shelter, Fort Lyon, had been a prison when I first fell ill. Before that it was a VA hospital, and before that a mental institution, and before that a cavalry fort, the one from which the Sand Creek Massacre was launched in 1864. A hundred and fifty women and children and elderly peace-minded men of the Cheyenne and Arapaho tribes were slaughtered in a matter of hours. The stables where the cavalry's horses had been fed and watered stood in back of the fort, the oldest buildings on the site. Colorado Coalition for the Homeless was bussing people into the fort from around the state: Grand Junction, Pueblo, Trinidad. They needed teachers. I needed a change.

Before I signed up I paid a visit to my psychologist, Carolyn, a worldly woman in her seventies who dressed sharp as a dart. She settled tidily into a plush chair and crossed her legs. I told her I hoped a month among people who'd suffered extremities of loss might help me to feel less alone. Teaching at the homeless shelter might make me feel useful.

I had a good home with Elisa, but disability is a well-traveled road to homelessness. I thought also of those nineteenth century Ugly Laws: if you were disabled displaying yourself on the street, you were presumed to be begging. My own trauma had been easier, so far, than that of the residents at Fort Lyon, but that didn't mean I didn't have plenty to learn from people so intimate with loss.

"I worry you'll be lonely at the shelter," Carolyn said. "You might feel very lonely, even abandoned."

I barely listened. "I'm lonely *here*."

When I first started talking to Carolyn, I'd faked a kind of bonhomie in her office until I started to feel myself really becoming that way around her, and then around others. It was probably medicinal. And it freed me up to expand our catalogue of subjects. It was Carolyn who first told me about John Speke, marooned on an island of Lake Tanganyika in 1858, spear tip of the imperialist assault. Speke convinced himself an insect had flown into his ear, one that began "with exceeding vigor, like a rabbit at a hole, to dig violently away at my tympanum." Maybe it did. Anyway, he stabbed himself in the eardrum to cure it.

But was it a bug? Tinnitus often manifests as a clicking, a sensation of fullness in the ear. Speke was partially blind by then and so needed his hearing to navigate himself off the island (and to map future sites of British plunder). Before that ringing, all he would have heard was the sound of lake water lapping a shore, the coos of doves interwoven with less familiar birds, the harmless buzz of insects with beautiful names: *nyenje, usubi, nyuki.*

Within a week of arriving at Fort Lyon I'd been laid low, but not by my ears. It was the food. The same food the residents gratefully lined up to raven down. Some of them hadn't been able to count on a meal in years. Meanwhile, my system was pampered by home cooking. Entrees that couldn't be easily named—greasy pasta, say, heaped under sugary meat—were new to me. I was learning what the residents already knew: if they served something you liked, get seconds and horde it—you didn't know what might happen next. Spoon what you could into a mug or fold it into one of the papery bathroom towels.

Although the administration forbid taking food out of the kitchen, you had to break that rule. The Colorado Coalition for the Homeless, under whose auspices Fort Lyon dubbed itself a "supportive residential community," had instituted any number of regulations: most websites were inaccessible from their online system, all prescription drugs had to be dispensed by staff, and married couples were forbidden to share a room.

"It's better than the Salvation Army for sure," explained one of the residents. "Salvation Army makes you pray on command and keep your top button buttoned . . ."

"No, no," an older resident cut him off. "There's no comparison with stuff like that. This place is paradise. This is paradise."

I wondered if they had something to settle my stomach in paradise. I left my room and walked through the subbasement tunnel that connected all four of the biggest dorms. First I passed a row of empty classrooms, then a long hall to the library, dogleg past rows of brass mailboxes that used to connect the ancient fort to the outside world, empty hospital rooms, a nonworking kitchen, up the elevators to Building 5.

The fort was over three hundred acres wide. I'd been given a master key. Outside the residential barracks I made a habit of trying every door, and behind them I found stacks of rusted wheelchairs, broken crutches, remnants of the shuttered hospital. Other rooms were stacked with gurneys, ancient X-ray machines. Here and there you'd find signs of squatters: an L-shaped closet with a stained mattress and a stack of candy wrappers, Tupperware.

The main hall in the main building was usually pop-
ulated, though, because the offices lay at one end and the
mess at the other. The clinic was located toward the front,
its door cracked open. My phone told me it was 4:45
p.m.; it was Friday, and the clinic would close any moment for the weekend. I spotted a woman at the counter
and she looked up, startled.

"Are you a resident?" she asked.

"I'm a teacher."

"But do you live here?"

"Temporarily."

"Everyone's here temporarily."

She couldn't break the rules. All of the residents at
Fort Lyon had been addicted to some kind of drug before they arrived there—addiction was a prerequisite—
and the infirmary had to keep strict paperwork, even if
all I wanted was Pepto-Bismol. She told me if I was sick
I should drive into town.

"But I don't have a car."

"There'll be a bus tomorrow afternoon."

I gave up on feeling any better as I walked from the
clinic and across the quad back to my room, hardly taking in
the view to which I'd become accustomed. Down the path
to the main road, a high row of hay bales concealed the out-
buildings of an unused farm. Sagebrush had blown there,
got trapped, blocked the passages. The first signs of life I
came across one early morning exploring were live chickens
in a coop behind the stables, ducks in another. I thought I'd
imagined them. My new friend Cas told me that one of the
other residents scattered chicken feed twice a day.

Cas was a gossip, which I liked. He was reorganizing the large library room downstairs between sessions engraving nudes in the art room (from memory, for the time being, but Cas was a charmer). "Cas is a con man," one woman told me, a woman who'd met her share. There's a parallel universe where Cas emcees a nightly show in Vegas and another where he emcees the same show in the Catskills. He's short and muscular and talks at speed.

He stopped me on the way back to my room to tell me all about a vintage *Captain America*, I think, that he'd found on a bench and that was worth too much ever to sell, and I cut him off. I told him that I needed to find a quiet place to vomit. He understood and he'd catch up with me later, but was there anything he could do? Well, would he mind spreading the word I was looking for some kind of cure?

Within the hour I was peeling open a packet of bismuth tablets. I learned that things often worked that way among residents: you put the word out about what you needed and maybe it found its way back to you. As for electrolytes, these were too valuable to hand off free but, Cas pondered, gosh, there were a couple of fellas who ran an informal dry goods out of the room one floor above my own. Did I know anything about it?

By the next day I was back to my typical morning ritual: wake, rise, shoes, sweatshirt, grab toothbrush, thermos, razor, don't forget keys, ensure door's locked, bathroom down the hall, brush, shave, and back in the room, return my keys to the table beneath the tacked-up paper in my handwriting that reads "Take Keys."

Speed and efficiency mattered. I was friendly and the residents were lonely—I was lonely too—but I don't like to talk before I've brushed my teeth. Fort Lyon was the Carlyle Hotel of shelters, but even there it took discipline to remain hygienic. The bathrooms in Building 8 were bereft of soap; you had to bring your own and keep it carefully. One of the residents, insufficiently medicated, squeezed the bottles down the sink. There were no counselors on site.

On my first week I addressed the crowd at a community meeting. This was the way I'd introduce myself, the path by which I'd become something other than a stranger to them. At the podium, I registered a little boredom on the faces around me, and also suspicion. Who was this interloper, neither resident nor staff, patient nor nurse.

I opened by talking about my ears, about the fact that my hearing and balance were going. Straightaway, the crowd uncrossed their arms. I was telling them—deliberately, I'd calculated this—that while of course I did not know what it was to suffer homelessness, at least I wasn't oblivious to pain. Of the language of pain, although I possessed no fluency, I could understand and speak a little. And that I was desirous of learning. I would know how to listen.

Dramatic loss is traumatic loss. Trauma breeds anxiety, depression. One resident, Jaime, who formerly used drugs to soothe his nerves, worked up the courage to talk to someone at a Denver shelter, get an application for up to two years at Fort Lyon, climb on the bus in Denver, and ride four hours east; on reaching the fort, he felt that old anxiety quicken. I understood. When my ride dropped me off at that half-abandoned cluster of institutional buildings hours from home and I heard the metal fire door of my room fall shut behind me, I too felt anxious. It would be another month until Elisa arrived to collect me. Why shouldn't the place make Jaime anxious too?

There's a brief questionnaire social workers administer to determine the level of trauma in someone's childhood. Ten questions measure three categories: abuse (physical, sexual), neglect (Did you go hungry? Were your parents addicted to drugs?), and household dysfunction (Were family members imprisoned? Was your mother beaten?). More than half of the people who take the test score less than 4 on this scale. For example, I score a 3 and my wife a 0. My four closest friends score a 2, a 1, a 3, and a 0. (Interestingly, those friends with higher scores—even at this low end—tend to be medicated against depression or anxiety; they get into trouble more, reach a little faster for that drink.) Jaime, based purely on what he felt comfortable sharing from his life, had to be well over a 6 or a 7.

"I can't tell people about the things that happened to me," Jaime said. "I mean, I can't bring myself to. Like, when I was a kid my dad used to pick me up and swing me around by the ears. It hurt like you couldn't believe it."

Score any higher than a 4 on this test and, statistically, you're four times more likely to develop an addiction, to fall victim to domestic violence. Your risk of chronic health problems escalates. Your risk of early death does too. The chances of heart disease, emphysema, and obesity all rise.

Another phenomenon becomes more statistically likely. You begin to blame yourself, in much the same way abusers have likely been blaming you for years.

Jaime said, "My dad would beat me up and I feel guilty about that. You tell people that, they think, 'Well what'd you do to make him?' You know, people blame you for what happened to you. I was in foster care and people say, 'Well you must have been a bad kid.' Or if they don't say it, they *think* it."

I met Jaime in a class I taught each afternoon in a room behind the groundskeeper's office: a long table and some ailing plants. I'd give him a prompt and he'd make something beautiful out of it right away, at least when he was able to make it to class. He worked in the mess hall most afternoons and aggressively applied himself. "I love it when people tell me I'm doing a good job," he told me in the hall on his way there. "They weren't sure what to do with the space by the window and I said, 'Well, what if we had a salad bar?' And they said yes, and it's just great—and now it's my space. Then people ask me, 'How about fruit?' So I get my hands on some."

When Jaime and I would talk after class, he came across as impossibly sweet. Though he's over thirty and plenty smart, he isn't confident about anything. I kept thinking of Jaime as younger than he was because he seemed so frightened. He keeps to himself, hides his ears inside headphones, speaks soft and shy.

"My brother . . ." he'd start and pause. Jaime was agitated, undermedicated. He looked afraid. "He was smoking crack and he'd just take things. He took things from my mother—my mother's an alcoholic and didn't notice half the time—and my brother took things from me, cleaned me out. I tried to get him to quit, but he kept saying, 'You don't know what it's like. You gotta try it.' So I smoked crack with him. I figured it'd make him comfortable, make him feel like he could listen to me, and then I'd work on getting him sober, trying to help him to change."

In and out of institutions for thirty years (foster care, shelters) it's hard to look at Jaime and conclude anything other than he never had a chance. And yet by the standards of Fort Lyon's new arrivals, Jaime wasn't doing badly. When residents first arrived at the fort and submitted to intake (clothes laundered, mandatory shower, paperwork) they often resembled the sort of people you see in news photographs emerging from explosions. Their world *had* exploded—they'd lost everything.

Homelessness traumatizes its victims. We might even call it a triple trauma. First, your life falls apart: family and friends shut their doors; your belongings disappear; your life, as you knew it, is over. This is a kind of living death. Then you're traumatized again, separately but relatedly, by the stress of living in danger. Shelters are lousy with drugs and violence; streets are cold and any of your possessions perpetually imperiled. You're disdained by your fellow man. You're lucky if the despair doesn't drive you to addiction, but addiction will be a third kind of trauma when it comes.

I grew increasingly able to spot new arrivals. Residents who'd been around for a few weeks or more were generally indistinguishable from the staff, but new residents still had the dull, haunted look of sleeplessness in their eyes, the postures of paranoia. They kept their heads down, wore bruises and cuts, seemed ready to bolt.

Rose, a woman I met in the hall by administration, still shook from acute withdrawal. Her hair was either brown or unwashed; her skin was that of a woman of sixty, though she was likely no older than forty-five.

I pulled up a chair beside her, slowly, then asked her what she was reading—she had Jeannette Walls's *The Glass Castle* in her hands—and from there, haltingly, she got on to the subject of waitressing.

"Seven years I was a waitress," she said, looking up whenever footfalls sounded in the hall. "I never thought I'd be homeless but it happened fast. Like, it was lightning fast. I stayed at the shelter in Grand Junction on and off for two years, whenever I needed a shower or a meal. But you wouldn't want to sleep there—it was an awful place: people shooting up in the bathroom, people angry at the world, all kinds of bad emotion. You *get* angry at the world, though; you'd get real suspicious of people, really anxious. I never felt calm for two years."

This is typical. Fort Lyon aims to provide a different model. Their philosophy holds that until you separate yourself from the fear you've been living in, the chronic stress, you won't be physically capable of addressing your situation or, frankly, doing anything rational.

Fight-or-flight responses, in the long term, change our blood pressure, release hormones like corticotropin and cortisol which, in sufficient quantity, inflect our mental state, often drastically. Our sense of empathy withdraws, and so does our self-esteem. The American Psychological Association lists anxiety, insomnia, muscle pain, high blood pressure, and a weakened immune system among the effects of chronic stress. Military veterans, people addicted to drugs, and survivors of sexual abuse are among the victims, and the Fort Lyon residents were often all three.

Presumably, they're not going to get any better in the same environments where they suffered. Therefore, the theory runs, Fort Lyon is right to collect them, wrest them out of the cities where they slept on the street and collected scorn. "I'm used to cities," one woman told me, a woman originally from Alaska. What cities had she lived in? "Oh well, Wasilla for a while. It's not big like real big, but the mountains keep you company. And Grand Junction in Colorado. But this . . ." She gestured out a window, beyond which rose the red brick of Building 5, but I knew she meant something else; she meant the fields beyond Building 5, fields that kept rolling dry and low until Missouri. It seemed desolate to me too. There were small cities in this part of eastern Colorado, but you'd need to drive nearly an hour to reach one. There used to be sugar beets in the farms, then there was ranching, now all hopes rest on a brewery being constructed by outside money. Meanwhile, aside from a handful of hog lots, little stirred.

There's a shuttle that runs to La Junta, the nearest town of any size. On my second Saturday morning I climbed aboard at 7 a.m. and asked the driver what the weather was going to be.

"Well," he said, stroking his goatee, making a show of philosophizing, "right now it's cold."

A voice from the back: "Possibly a little bit of moisture, which means we ain't gettin' shit."

I'd seen some of the landscape on the four-hour drive there from Denver: shotgun houses, prefab stables, silos. I knew there were rattlesnakes along the dirt roads. On one of my anxious walks around the place a local pulled up beside me in his Chevy truck and said, "Damn, boy, you gotta be careful, there's rattlers out here. Rolled over this one just a half mile back. You want to feel the rattle? Go on, he can't hurcha anymore."

That Sunday I wanted to find a good breakfast. The only eggs I saw at the Fort were powdered and I saw them only once. I looked up "La Junta restaurants" from one of the two old Department of Corrections desktop PCs at the Fort Lyon library and I found what I wanted: Copper Kitchen.

Owner Larry Tanner grabbed my hand when I came in the door and squeezed on the bones like I owed him money, but in a friendly way. "Welcome! Where you from? What brings you into town?"

He wore a waxed mustache and spoke with command. "They sent you to give us a good write-up? Well, you talk us up now because we want that Fort to stay open. Have you been down there yet? Well, you meet those people and they just got opened right up. They got the Lord in 'em. You'll see it. They got the light of the Lord and they start to use their talents and they just change completely."

He's right that residents often transform during their stay, but that transformation is less apotheosis than relaxation, a falling back into the people they'd like to be, rather than the people they've been forced to become. The people they can be when they aren't holding their breath.

About halfway through the month I was invited to dinner at the home of one of the politicians who'd made the place possible. She lived with her husband, the town judge, in a Spanish-style manse. Outside, the plains descended to a ravine where bluestem and barley grew and rabbits ran through it. Inside the manse a palm tree rose from the dining room's center, fed sunlight from a glass roof.

Straightaway we tucked into a dinner of roast chicken and greens and country bread, washing it down with glasses of cold water. As I ate I told them all about Jaime, how his childhood had so filled him with anxiety and so starved him for kindness he had trouble simply being in the world.

The judge shook his head. "There's no doubt," he told me, "Some people start off with more of a challenge. But at a certain point, your fate is in your own hands."

But what about the trauma test? What about the fact that some people reach adulthood with the odds hard against them, that they have to fight so much harder than people, like me, who were fed every night?

As the judge spoke, I had to strain to hear him. "I haven't met Jaime. But taking responsibility is a part of the recovery process. Yes, some people aren't fortunate, but the person ultimately responsible for where you are right now is you. Take Randy here . . ."

The judge indicated the gangly twentysomething eating dinner across from us. I'd known he wasn't their son, but the nature of his relationship to the judge wasn't clear.

"Randy's had some problems, but he managed to find his way to us and he's working on knowing what's best for himself now. He and I have been talking about responsibility."

The hostess clarified a little: "Randy met my husband in court a few times and he needed some guidance, but he's a good man. He just went around with the wrong crowd."

Randy started to speak—I caught the word "follower"—but the judge interrupted, "Randy, look people in the eye when you talk to them." His voice advertised patience more than warmth. The voice said, *I'll be patient for a while yet.*

"I work at the hog farm now," the boy said. He'd had to put a number of sick animals "in the box" that day—the box was filled with carbon monoxide. "You feel bad doing it sometimes, but you can't risk the others getting sick too." He talked about his job for a few minutes with slow care, knowing the judge was listening.

And then the judge was laughing. "Maybe John's heard enough about that."

We walked outside in time to see an owl swoop down over the barley grass, probably in search of a baby rabbit.

I turned over what the judge had said about responsibility. I was reminded of Mr. Bridge in Evan S. Connell's classic story, "The Beau Monde of Mrs. Bridge." A businessman who impatiently explains to his wife, "You take all the people on earth and divide up everything, and in six months everybody would have just about what they have now."

I thought about Ronald Green, who wound up addicted to drugs and homeless after his wife of thirty-two years was killed by a drunk driver ("He crossed over the lane, pushed the steering wheel right up through her chest, through my baby's chest"). Unprompted, not knowing who I might be, he invited me into his room for homemade ham and beans, saying, "You want some any time, just ask; I don't want you going hungry." It was a spontaneous gift and he willingly gave it. That was common at Fort Lyon. It seemed to express something the residents knew to be true about life. I suspected it accounted for why some of them were there—they weren't cutthroat enough to make their way in the world.

But maybe I was wrong. As economist Robert Frank describes in his book *Success and Luck*, small amounts of early luck matter hugely as time goes on. There's a name for this phenomena, "the Matthew Effect," after a quotation of Jesus's in Matthew 25:29: "For unto everyone that hath shall be given, and he shall have abundance; but from him that hath not shall be taken away even that which he hath."

The sociologist who coined the term, Robert K. Merton, had been studying the distribution of acknowledgement and awards in scientific research. He found that in team projects, the more well-known scientists were given a disproportionate share of the credit for the results, even if their more obscure colleagues had done more of the work.

It's important to note that the more famous scientists don't need to do anything sinister or unethical for the Matthew Effect to work. All they have to do is be more famous. It isn't bird-dogging—stealing someone else's data or taking credit for their idea—but something more structural, imperturbable: it's luck perpetuating luck.

Frank provides a few even stranger examples. Paraphrasing a pair of studies, one in the *Economics of Education Review*, another in the *Journal of Labor Economics*, he describes how the youngest students in a given year of school are less likely to hold student leadership positions. They're simply a bit less mature—not dramatically so—but small differences matter. "Other studies have found that even after controlling for cognitive ability and other psychological and physical traits, students who hold leadership positions go on to earn significantly higher wages." Are we to assume early trauma is less meaningful than month of birth? Are we to assume the tendency to blame one's self doesn't compound? It did for me.

I thought of the homeless man we found lying in the center of a busy street one night in Denver. He was conscious but drunk, begged us to leave him alone, let him be run over and killed. We carried him to the curb, me and a couple of strangers walking by. Once we'd got him off the street, he stood up, cursed at us, and staggered back into traffic, lay down there.

Sometimes regret is a small thing. But the mind sights it like a bird dog and runs.

I thought of my own father's unhappiness, that long story he'd pour whiskey and tell me twice a week for twenty years: the trouble making friends because his family moved so often; the fear and loneliness in Vietnam (and the mysteries of his conscience—the things I'll never learn about Cambodia); then the scandal with his business and unresolvable anger; the temper he took out on me. I think of the fire I built him one afternoon, the hand he put on my shoulder ("Don't expect me around in the future," he said. "I won't be here"). His meaning was clear: he was thinking of killing himself.

He told me he fought hard as a boy and fought hard as a man, and it still wasn't enough. He said I was a screwup for not fighting harder, not seeing enemies for what they were. And if I couldn't learn to fight harder, and fast, I'd be lost. Life afforded no pause. Slack your pace and you're finished.

Then my body got sick. Who do you fight when your enemy is yourself?

I lashed out at my luck; it had never been good. How could it ever turn around?

I had never been to a meeting of Alcoholics Anonymous. I didn't even know such a thing was allowed. My only direct experience of AA was driving my dad to meetings at my hometown church, then reading for an hour in the park across the street to make sure he stayed inside.

One of my closest friends among the Fort Lyon residents, Nancy, had grown up in a famously wealthy Connecticut town across the state from my own home-town. Her father, an industrialist, had lost their fortune, and two of her three brothers developed addictions. So did Nancy.

"I only drank when I couldn't get codeine," she told me one evening as Jaime set out last night's leftovers behind us. If it hadn't been for AA, she said, she'd still be looking through dumpsters for carelessly discarded pills. "If you want to understand the people here," she said, "you've got to come with me tonight. When they go around the room just say, 'My name is John,' and don't say anything else. But it's an open meeting so anyone can come—you aren't breaking any rules." She smirked, perhaps seeing the suggestion made me nervous.

We walked to the meeting room together in the 8:30 p.m. dark of early spring. I'd gone quiet, worried about saying or doing the wrong thing while I was there, as though it were a sacred occasion.

And it was a sacred occasion. Sitting in the converted gymnasium where the meeting was held, beneath a large plaque bearing the names of the residents who had died in the last two years, I felt both the solemn restlessness I'd felt on Sunday mornings as a kid and the worried watchfulness of someone who hasn't done their homework. All the while I kept as quiet as Nancy had told me to keep and listened as carefully as I could.

Alcoholics Anonymous and Narcotics Anonymous do great work at Fort Lyon, holding at least one meeting every night. AA is necessary because there isn't funding for formal counselors. Even if there were, getting mental health professionals out to Las Animas would be a trick. When, like Jaime, residents shy from AA, they have no formal program to guide them, no addiction counseling on site. The recovery program at Fort Lyon is AA or nothing.

The next night, at dinner, I joined my friends Nancy and Cas at their table in the mess hall. A third man about my age was there. He was quiet, disaffected, absently putting away his food. I never caught his name, and the staff was stacking plates not far away, muddying the sound— but I'll call him Carl.

My experience with Carl was a strange one. He was leaving the fort to join a friend in Missouri with whom he was writing a book. I asked him if Missouri was home, or once had been.

"No, I'm from Boston. Grew up there and went to school there."

Carl wasn't particularly interested in talking with me, but I was interested in talking with Carl—Fort Lyon was a long way from Boston. I'd gone to school there too, Emerson College as a clueless undergraduate. I told him so.

"Oh yeah, that's where I went too," he said, betraying no surprise. "It would have been a few years before you, but I lived in a dorm they closed down just after—weird old hotel called the Charlesgate."

It was then I noted that Carl was wearing an Emerson College T-shirt, a gray one with faded lettering. Why hadn't I seen it before?

"When *I* lived in Charlesgate," I said, "I had a view of the Storrow overpass."

For maybe a second he was stirred. "Oh?" he said. "I had that view too. We had the corner room on floor three."

I know the room. A good friend had lived there only a few years after Carl. And here Carl and I were—two decades later—having both slept the night in that corner room, both anxious about our first year at college, a year in which we both drank a lot.

"I was a stand-up comedian," he said, naming a troupe whose shows I'd been to see. "A lot of comedians drink, and lots of them are more fun when they drink. But I wasn't more fun."

He cleared his tray—said something about having things to pack for Missouri—and disappeared down the hall. Cas and Nancy were talking about Cas's daughter ("She is my absolute best friend. Remind me to show you a picture—she's just the best"). I disappeared too, into an empty office. I made some notes about our conversation until the stillness of the room and the emptiness of that floor of the building made me restless. I entered a hallway I shouldn't have entered and wound up in the infirmary, abandoned for evening. There were a few haphazard stretchers lining the hall, an empty oxygen tank. One translucent window flickered with light. I heard a scrape from upstairs.

Walking back to my room alone that night, in the kind of uncompromising wind you find on the plains, I realized then that I was not merely touched by anxiousness but panicked. My breath went short, my fingers numbed. I knew I had to fight or run but instead of either I froze up.

The depths of my hypocrisy were being sounded. Like a lot of people, I've often nodded along when someone else explained that homelessness *could happen to anyone.* I'd piously mumble assent. But I'd never believed it. That's what I learned on my nervous walk around the empty playground and abandoned farm inside Fort Lyon's walls: I'd never really believed it. I'd felt, past tense—in the same way we all feel immortal in our youth—as though I'd manage to escape the worst no matter what. Yes, *it could happen to anyone,* but most of those to whom the worst occurs either never had a chance or let their guard down at a crucial time, which I most assuredly would not do.

But it wasn't so. The fear that gnawed at me when I sped my pace to exhaust myself is what every one of the other residents had felt not once but often—it was the fear they lived inside.

Here's the part that seemed irrational and still does: I wasn't just afraid because I understood now that anyone could suffer what the residents suffered. I was afraid the moment of disaster for myself had taken place *already*, that my life, as I knew it, was gone.

In the following days the fear kept gnawing, taught me lessons that may have been lies. The fear told me that Denver was not my home anymore, that I wouldn't be welcomed back. Had Elisa and my friends already deserted me, or was it a matter of time? Had my family in the Midwest and Southwest and New England shut their doors? I'm a sadder person than I used to be, quieter. When things go wrong I order a drink. How much do I like that drink? Enough to lose everything if it seems as though everything is losing me?

I knew, of course, that I wasn't abandoned, but I also didn't know. I called Elisa and some friends and family with my expensive headphones and tried to make myself heard through the wind as it bent the trees and scattered twigs across my path. But no one could fathom the fear.

I weighed what kept me from permanent residence at Fort Lyon and it didn't weigh much. Yes, I had a family, but my parents were getting older and my sister was far away with kids to raise. My wife and I loved each other, but I took her goodwill for granted. Illness and deafness kept me from staying in better touch with friends. The hours I worked earned me less.

It was in this way I came to better understand the terrifying positions of the people behind the lit windows of the strongholds I circled. Yes, it would take time for everything to fall apart, but it wouldn't feel like it took time.

And of course Elisa did arrive, in a way that Jaime's mother, Cas's ex-wife, and Rick's children wouldn't arrive for them. She came to collect me in our Subaru and Cas went out to meet her. They were friends by the time I joined them. On the way out he gave me a picture he'd painted one night in jail: a slithery tree out of a swords-and-sorcery comic with a valiant prince and lithesome maid.

"I used M&M's to paint it. You can get some in jail sometimes and you just put them in a little cup until the dye washes off and that tints the water. Use a couple of toothbrush bristles to make your brush."

I felt weird driving away from the place, a place where I'd been sheltered, fed, benignly neglected by the administration, and taken care of by the residents. On a stop for dinner, Elisa caught me slipping some of the burger joint's free mustard packets into my pocket.

"Are you *stealing* those? Do you need mustard on the ride?"

I started to say, "I'm taking them for my room," but stopped myself and shook my head. We'd planned to stay a night in Pueblo on the way home. The first night in our hotel room we fought about money and I was defensive. We made up in the morning, but as we left the hotel I walked slowly, concentrating on the postures of everyone around me, their clothes, their expressions.

"What is it, sweetie?" Elisa asked.

"It's that everyone's got somewhere to go," I said. "They're *fashionable* too."

"Fashionable?"

"They look vigorous. It's strange."

Something else struck me. I'd been able to hear better in Fort Lyon. Not well, by my prior lights, but maybe not quite so badly as in the years that immediately preceded. I'd felt difficult lows—whole evenings when I couldn't hear even the sound of my own fist tapping a wall—but I hadn't felt as many as only a month before.

The loud reverberation in my head hadn't lessoned. On the other hand I hadn't used a cane at the fort. I'd brought one along but hadn't needed to touch it. The room spun around me on two separate nights but only two. And each time it came to a stop after a couple of hours.

How much of this was the condition finally, after impossible years, coming to retract its claws? And how much was my body adapting—learning to work with the machines in my ears, learning to better interpret the sounds they provided? How much was my body learning to compensate for the impairment of my balance?

And how should I live—how should I regulate my emotional life, my expectations of the world—when health could be given or taken away so capriciously? When it might worsen again at any moment, or might hold off indefinitely? When so much that mattered rode the currents of fate? Or of luck?

Lost Things Dreams

In July of 2017 we stayed at the Jamaica Plain apartment of a music teacher. It smelled like untreated wood in a damp climate. Outside the windows ascended a warren of other apartments: lit stained glass; night-quiet brick; trees in the courtyard, half obscured by rails; either somebody was moving behind a gate or the dark leaves caught the wind.

Elisa's company would have preferred we move back completely—I wanted to do this; I had connections in Boston—but Elisa didn't like Boston. It was cloistered, cold. That's why we'd moved west years ago, to the sort of desert air that made her feel at home. Instead of a transfer, she and the company cut a deal for a month on-site. We found a place in our old neighborhood. African instruments rusticated in corners of the apartment: stretched skins and gut-strung bows and tensed branches arched into harps.

Our first night back we ate sushi outdoors on Center Street. In the manner of a five-year absence the old neighborhood was changed and not changed. I felt guilty: I hadn't been here to look after the place.

Guilt seemed to me a distinct psychological stage, like denial. When my condition became unmanageable, I wondered if somehow, in some lost quarter of my past, I'd called all of this down upon myself. Was it the cigarettes I smoked in college? The mystery pills a schizophrenic friend once dared me to take? Worse: was it the nights I'd wasted, idly reading, or fumbling around in the dark with girls when I ought to have been . . . and here I didn't know—doing something for *the economy*? Thanks to my breeding and conditioning, I assumed for a time it was my lack of riches that made me guilty. To be rich is to feel *safe from feeling*, as Elizabeth Daryush puts it in her poem "Children of Wealth." In the nights I'd lain sick at home, on my back, slowly spinning, I'd searched all the dark corners for the missed step, the mistake of living among people when I ought to have lived among *opportunities*. I laid careful plans for how I'd get it right next time, start from the beginning. There was a right world, a world where I hadn't gotten sick, hadn't lost those years, but I'd missed the turn, hadn't arrived on time, could never arrive.

Or perhaps this was what Heidegger and Sartre called the wages of *bad faith*, the knowledge I'd put off all the meaningful decisions I might have made until too late, that I'd lived my life provisionally, always at school. Always with my nose in a book.

All that thinking was gone by June of 2017. Fort Lyon had made real for me the role of luck, solidified nebulous ideas. If we have secure childhoods, we grow up assuming the world is coherent. This is an error: the world is contingent, as are the bodies from which we can't separate, the bodies we are. This childish desire to return to some imagined, coherent place is what embroils us in crackers religions, conspiracy theories, what gets us buying books about disaster that shellac virtue onto luck (the guy blown apart by a bomb who writes a book about how it's only made him stronger—all change being change for the better—bunk like that). There's a whole industry devoted to imposing false order on real chaos, but we consume its products at our own risk. If the universe is ordered, but we fall out of place with that order (we fall sick, we fall apart) then we're the element that doesn't belong, or else we've called this upon ourselves. No, Providence did not take my hearing and my balance to reprove me of some transgression in this life or the last life. Life does not guarantee rewards to those who "work hard and play by the rules," and it never has. The only good is kindness, and nature doesn't urge it on us.

Elisa and I talked about this over the sushi, and about the weird guilt. Elisa ordered lemon in the salmon rolls and it was an excellent move. I said the guilt about the neighborhood was probably a good thing—it meant I wasn't riddled with guilt about myself. It's what was left after I'd quit feeling responsible for the thing that had happened to my ears.

She nodded, lemon and salmon in her mouth. "Good progress, good progress."

We walked around Jamaica Pond after dinner, late sun against the far shore. I'd gone jogging there in my twenties but I couldn't force that to mean anything. The past wasn't a real past, partially because there was no way to make it a triumph story. I'd left Boston a promising author of a debut novel. I'd left friends behind. Some had moved away; from others I'd grown distant. I had a meeting lined up to formally shutter the arts review site I'd informally quit when I got sick. Most of the time I could keep all this in my head without mourning it but, that accomplished, I couldn't make it mean anything. I was between narratives. I didn't have a story for myself. Everything came apart when I fell ill; now I was a little better, for no understandable reason, and could fall ill again at any time, for no understandable reason. Biology wanted me to dwell on this, to constantly review it: the amygdala is surrounded by the hippocampus—our flight-or-fight-or-freeze responses surrounded by the part of our brain that controls narrative memory. Who was this self of mine—what was his story?

That night we heard drumming. It sounded like djembes. Drumming and pause. Drumming and a longer pause. The percussive character of the sound makes it a kind of music that reproduces through my Widex Dream aids. In fact, what I heard was little different than what I would have heard before my ears went bad. It was the same sound with the hearing aids off or on, just softer. Its vibrations hung in the air.

. . .

The reading room at the Widener Library was thick with diligence. A girl with acne bit her lip as she wrote, smiled. A pale boy with the eyes of a sociopath set huge headphones in place. Someone pulled the cap of a highlighter. Someone tilted their head, crooked to read their own cursive straight. They looked like those pictures you see of NASA engineers during a launch: reflection of pearl-blue screens on bifocals. A white-haired woman lowered and then rose her head as she walked down the central aisle, as though it were a difficult thing for her to walk down an aisle alone, or as though she'd just come across something in her reading that had put all her previous ideas in disorder and she had to be careful not to send them spinning around the room.

Unaffiliated with a good research library in Colorado, I had vowed to make the most of my time in Boston, where an old card let me wander the Widener stacks. There were five miles of books in those stacks. Widener felt like one of the navels of the world: folios of cuneiform from Turkish typesetters, Sanskrit scrolls, a perfect Gutenberg Bible under glass in a little room where a passel of business-suited VIPs ate pâté from Cardullo's and talked about . . . fundraising? Netflix?

I made for the stacks alone and took armfuls of stuff back to the reading room: *The Correspondence of Jonathan Swift*, bound medical journals, bound volumes of *Swift Studies*, *Hygëia: or Essays Moral and Medical*, *The Routledge History of Disease*, a notebook full of passwords and URLs I could only access through Widener's alumni-access portholes. I knew who I resembled, snaking to a free chair in the back, guarding my laptop—there were two kinds of people at the reading room: expensively dressed undergraduates and disheveled adults. I include the faculty here. The average undergraduate at Widener might have been wearing a Harvard T-shirt, but the sneakers on their feet cost four hundred dollars and their postures were eerily straight. The average adult slunk or scuttled in, hunched, arms full of bags full of books, and spent the day crawling the stacks like a spider. I used to see them a decade ago and wonder *what the hell*. Now I was one of them: visible impairment (the hearing aids), curved back of the chronic reader, my frame too thin. It was fine. I was at home.

My job that month—a job both necessary and self-imposed—was to learn all I could about Ménière's disease, the history of the thing, the wrong directions, divisions, generations of secret infirmity, disbelief. In order to digest it, I needed a friend. Ideally, this friend would have endured everything I'd endured. Ideally, he'd be articulate, accessible, free with his time. Jonathan Swift was the only real choice. I wanted, also, to see what end he'd come to. I wanted to look my own possible end in the eye—to see what might be waiting, however absurd.

I turned pages, learning about him: his moods, famous cheapness, tender love for a former student, Stella, who he called *ppt*, "poor pretty thing" (James Joyce thought it must have made Swift feel incestuous, the former student part, and made cryptic fun of it in *Finnegans Wake*: "Peppt! That's rights, hold it steady!"). I saw in Swift's hopelessness the lines of my own life. I read about how

Oscar Wilde's father saw in Swift "the morose, discontented, and unhappy temper of some persons affected with deafness." In a neat bit of prejudice he contrasted "the frown of the partially deaf and the smile of the totally blind." I frowned over this. And I frowned over Swift's sense of humor, as I came to understand it; I too liked dirty jokes, but Jonathan Swift liked the wrong kinds of dirty jokes: coprology. Then again, the poor guy was prescribed dung pills as an emetic, a purging cure for his strain of Ménière's, a disease he didn't have a name for, but one that kept him up all night spinning, the way I'd been kept up for years and will be kept up again. (Swift to Stella: "Oh! Faith, I had an ugly giddy fit last night in my chamber, and have got a new box of pills to take, and hope I shall have no more this good while . . . one fit shakes me a long time.")

I reread *Gulliver's Travels*, this time with a pencil. I started writing onto the page when I reached the third and most various voyage of his adventures, the Isle of Luggnagg. There he's admitted to an audience with the king of the Luggnaggians, who receives him with ceremony and grants him lodgings in the capital. Once ensconced, Gulliver, as is his custom, makes every effort to learn what he can about this alien land and discovers, to his delight, a marvelous race, the Struldbruggs, a rare type of child granted the gift of immortality.

Gulliver is dazzled by this news. He can only imagine what a marvelous life this must be, to see the shapes of great oceans and rivers altered with time, kingdoms turned to ruin and obscure villages conquering all. "I should then see the Discovery of the *Longitude*, the *perpetual Motion*, the *Universal Medicine*, and many other great Inventions brought to the utmost Perfection," he perorates, wistfully.

But the Luggnaggians burst out laughing. The plight of the immortal Struldbruggs is nothing to envy. Gulliver had just made a mistake that many a traveler there had made as well. He was wrong to think ancient Struldbruggs could be happy, because such wishful thinking "supposed a Perpetuity of Youth, Health, and Vigor." As the Struldbruggs age and continue to age, it is explained, "the Diseases they were subject to still continue without increasing or diminishing." Past age eighty, their principal feeling is envy, particularly envy of "the Vices of the younger sort, and the Deaths of the old."

Language changes, as we know, from one age to another. Born in a bygone era, the Struldbruggs aren't able to converse with anyone under two hundred years old. "They lie under the Disadvantage of living like Foreigners in their own Country." They beg and nurse their miseries. What's left for them in life? Life has long moved on.

Back when I lived in Boston—back in 1999, the far past—I spent a lot of time listening to poetry aloud. The first time I walked into the Cantab Lounge was the night of the National Poetry Slam finals. A sly old devil with a handshake that could castrate bulls took my three dollars at the door and welcomed me as though I were a prodigal son. Everyone took turns reading, and when I stood up to read the folded pages I'd brought along—I remember the line "a basket of rain"—somehow the crowd stayed with me. When they clapped at the end, the host said they'd like to see me back the next week. "And bring a basket of rain!" It was the doorman with the ordnance grip. I'd found welcome, seemingly a whole room of it.

College had ended that spring, and until that night I hadn't known there was a club around the corner. A friend from class had invited me out dancing and I'd taken medium-strength drugs and made some friends. Black leather and slicked hair, right side of my face obscured by a maze drawn with eye-liner in the dark, I'd been having fun. I'd been kissed by a few strangers and the night was young.

I wasn't a gifted dancer. A friend on the floor with me said, "No, not like that. Try to imagine you're making love." Seconds later: "Oh wait, no, don't do that." Later, by the bar, it came out that I'd been writing some poems. "You've got to go to the Cantab," my friend said. "It's practically next door. Let's go now and come back in an hour."

So we wandered down the steps of a dive bar filled with Cambridge locals (people who actually worked, as distinct from Harvard types, though there were kids from non-Harvard schools) and into a room where I'd come to spend two years' worth of Wednesday nights. Folding chairs and small Formica tables would always wait around a slightly raised black stage with a single microphone. The sign-up list would always fill up fast. Judy at the bar would always pour the well drinks strong.

That night, a woman my age—she'd introduce herself as Melissa—sat at a corner table with what I remember as two separate binders full of poems. They were her own poems, and she and I started to flip through them and read them to each other, oblivious of the competition from the stage.

There are times when you feel attracted to a stranger simply because they're attracted to you. That was Melissa and me, both of us. We looked good together and people were good enough to note it. They'd tell us to get a room. But if *they* got a room, we decided, they wouldn't have to watch us. Later that summer we'd go night swimming at Walden Pond, dance close at clubs, and talk about the future not at all.

I'd only just met her—she'd just moved back to Boston from Ithaca—but Melissa made me proud when she reached the microphone that night. She looked at her notes and led us through our breathing by breathing herself, slowly. She backed away from the mic. The room settled back. She had that marvelous capacity to wave the room away and lure us into a kind of trance. How much of this was a put-on? And, in the context of performance poetry, does that question mean anything?

"Hush," she said. The title? It seemed to be a known poem among the construction-job kids in the back rows and big-heeled barflies—they hooted. There were nods and hums. "*All* right." "Mmm." Like some slam poets can do, she assumed authority by setting her shoulders, conjured the atmosphere of a Sunday service. We waited in attendance.

We knew the white folks and their kitchens
and bathrooms and broom-closets and their money.
We knew how to hold onto one other.

"Hush," she said, and she held the hush. Slam poetry, then thoroughly derided in academic circles, is about as close as our culture comes to the kind of half-chant epics Homer would have known, or that Parry and Lord found in the Serbo-Croatian folk songs of the 1930s. Done well, it can have the same effect—like the best music, it makes us complicit in its progress; like the best stories, it moves quick and bright.

And we hush.

A few weeks later, Melissa and I were drinking Turkish coffee at Café Algiers when one of her friends walked in, a man in his late twenties. She introduced him and I recognized his name.

"That's not surprising," the new guy said, "I'm a *rather* well-known poet."

Even after Melissa moved to New York and started teaching at Brooklyn College, I'd run into the rather well-known poet around Cambridge. Sometimes he pretended we hadn't met before. He symbolized this odd line of continuity for me—whatever I was doing in my life, he'd somehow be around.

"John?" He'd say "John Cotter? I know someone with the same name."

. . .

In Cambridge, in the summer of 2017, Elisa and I passed
that same well-known poet outside Central Square. His
hair looked like a rat ran through it. Elisa had met him
a few times but he didn't seem to recognize either of us,
just stormed forward, what seemed to be a *Miami Vice*-
style sports coat swirling around him, a size too large, in
a strong wind.

We were on our way to visit our old friend Chris at his
place in Cambridgeport. I wasn't surprised he'd moved
there because it was one of those places in Cambridge
where people like Chris lived, people who'd grown up
there all their lives: it was a neighborhood, not the trail-
ings of some university.

Were we all right with eating outside? There was a
back deck, a little yard. I asked for a white wine. Chris
didn't look ill, which was hugely refreshing because he'd
been gravely ill only a few years before. It had been
leukemia, acute lymphoblastic leukemia: one of those
phone calls after routine bloodwork where the doctor
tells you to drop everything, go right to the hospital,
check yourself in, expect to stay. Chris had a new baby,
Gus, but couldn't hold him; he was in isolation, visitors
had to wear masks—a month at Brigham and Women's
in Brookline, then another hospitalization for the bone
marrow transplant that ultimately saved his life. I sent
him a note when he fell ill but we had already grown
apart. While I wasted years with the spins in Colorado,
Chris was getting himself exposed to the same level of

radiation as a Chernobyl first responder, what someone on his medical team called a "kill dose."

There's a period of life—in my case, my late thirties, early forties—where every day it seems a new friend has gone mostly gray. Chris had gray stubble on his face; it made him suddenly unfamiliar. We were both changed but alive and somehow years had passed. I mentioned that we'd been snubbed by the rather well-known poet on the street outside.

"Oh, I know that guy," Chris said. "He's such a weird guy. In the '90s he was trying to convince me to be in this play he was directing, but the play would happen around people all the time without them knowing it was happening."

"He's always, like, impossibly disheveled," Elisa said, smiling with fondness. None of us could help but like the guy.

"You know I moved here in '94," I told Chris. "There used to be this other guy? He was mentally ill but maybe he was homeless too—you could never tell—who rode his bike everywhere and said *whoop whoop* and you could hear him like a Doppler effect in every part of town."

"I don't think that guy was homeless," Chris said. "Someone was looking after him. But hey, do you remember this guy—?" He stood, hunched his shoulders, stomped forward with his head like a ram. Instantly I knew the character he meant, although I hadn't seen quite this posture, quite that battering-ram walk in twenty years. It arrested me to remember a piece of the past like this, and it was even wonderful that Chris, separately—we hadn't known one another—had shared it. It formed a bubble of joy that rose from my chest to break in my throat, but it never reached my mouth, just kept rising, the way the corners of a room reset to spin during vertigo, without completing their circuit.

It was one of those heavy-air summers, like someone left the door to the steam room open. The pines in Chris's yard shuffled their needles. His wife, Rachel, brought food outside, something light and delicious. All the while Elisa was talking about compassion fatigue, how the president caused her stress ("He was committing treason again this morning; I wish he'd stop"), but she was okay, she was getting through her days, "until the slightest thing goes wrong in my own life, and then I can't handle it, I just fall apart."

I felt a drop of rain, and I experienced one of those moments of self-deception: it could be anything, it doesn't have to be a drop of rain. Then another: it will pass. But the Widex Dreams brought me the unmistakable sound of leaves pelted by fat drops. The sun had gone away, clouds loomed.

"I think this may be okay," Chris said. "Is this okay? Or maybe we should go in."

I wanted to eat in the rain if the rain didn't get any stronger; inside, noise would bounce off the walls, echo—I'd hardly hear. But I couldn't let my devices get wet. I took them off and slipped them into my pocket. Like I'd stuffed my ears with cotton, my friends went silent, only their lips in motion. The plates and knives scratched from away. Chris's voice was a voice from three backyards down the block. Sound measures distance, but in the presence of sound vibrations here I noticed the lack of delay: when Rachel and Elisa clinked their wineglasses together, the noise matched the image, but it shouldn't match because the noise was so far-off—it should have trailed the image if it was going to sound so faint.

The rain careened down; we gathered the plates in a rush.

In the evenings, when Elisa and I collapsed ourselves onto the apartment's couch, the heat from our bodies made it warmer still.

"I've been having the same dream every night," I told her. "You know, the one where you find a closet you never noticed, and inside are all these things you didn't remember you owned: your old jean jacket, a blanket from when you were a kid."

She spoke softly in response. She wasn't facing me—she was looking at an oud.

I said, "I didn't catch that. It's not your fault because—I don't think I've mentioned this to you before—but I have *hearing* problems."

Shocked, "You *do?*"

"I try to play it cool, but yeah. I'm hard of hearing."

She let her jaw fall open. "I had *literally* no idea."

"I'm so glad I've been able to play this off so smoothly."

I leaned in to kiss her and we wound up lying back on the couch together, her body wrapped in my arms.

Hearing aids complicate intimacy but it can be okay—
you just have to learn how to hold your head. It becomes
second nature: put the back of your head to the pillow;
don't rest on your right or left side unless you support
your head in a way that holds off the hinge-squeak of
feedback; make a tripod of your fingers around the ear to
give the machine space; you can brush your cheek against
your partner's, but only to a point; you can embrace them
completely, but there's a certain way you have to tilt your
head, hold your neck. You train yourself; you wouldn't
think any more to do things otherwise.

Eventually you grow less shy about it. In the same way,
I don't have shyness about asking restaurants for a seat
against the wall, or asking others at dinner to switch so I
can take sound in from one direction alone. Every place I
go in the evenings—bars, coffee shops, friends' houses—I
ask if we can sit outside. Often, indoor echoes are too
much. Often I nod and pretend. It's necessary to pretend.

In the bad days of the illness, E imposed a limit, for
her own sanity, on how often I could mention my ears.
When they're bad now, meaning I can hardly hear at all,
I tell her about it as a by-the-way, an incidental. What
at first struck me as lonely-making now feels like good
instinct, good training: I'm acting *as if.* I complain less to
myself now too. It is a stage that took a while to reach,
but I've arrived.

Most frustrations I feel now aren't with Elisa but with
strangers. And it's not the strangers I blame. To create a
bond of intimacy, we lower our voice. In a room full of
shouting kids, their mother will sotto voce the adult stuff

in my ear—she's establishing intimacy, wry mutuality—
but precisely because the kids are shouting, whatever she
tells me is lost. I say *what* and miss it a second time. I
never do find out.

Incidentals, the definition of low stakes, but still. My
favorite barista confides in me out of habit; we like each
other, we joke, so when I walk in he comes up to the
counter to confess out of range of his boss's hearing, out
of mind of the other patrons; he lowers his voice, even
moves his lips as little as he can get away with. Each time,
I remind myself it's the opposite of unfriendly—I'm invited to the conspiracy. But like a narc I say *I'm sorry?
What?* I tell him again that I'm hard of hearing and he
nods and says, "Me too." Lots of people do that. So you
amp it to "I'm deaf," and their fellow feeling diminishes
not at all. "Oh, totally, I'm deaf too." The word has no
meaning. The world remains an arm's length off.

Gossip, caveats—you miss these. A wave of the hand.
"It's not important," "It doesn't matter." Texture.

My life in whispers: James Bond films when I was a
kid (the mystery woman who warns him *you're in danger
here*); my mother, hushed, about what was wrong with
Peg ("It's *cancer*"); my mom and dad on Christmas Eve,
murmurs drifting upstairs (I heard the rustle of boxes in
paper being set beneath the tree, my father's low voice,
"*There's a lot this year*," and the way that thrilled me).

Loud bars are bad until they're really loud, almost un-
bearably loud, at which point they become good: if everyone's shouting at the top of their lungs, I can take off
my hearing aids and join the democracy. You can shout

the kinds of things in a loud bar you could never say in the quiet. You can shout like no one hears.

Insinuation, sex. The old man who sat down beside me on a bench with a drink on the Santa Monica pier. Like my barista, he barely moved his lips when he spoke (*"You're enough to drive Oscar Wilde"*). Action items I murmured into the throats of girls at clubs. Instructions in the dark. It wasn't that long ago. Stubbornly, it feels like I was someone else. I'm someone else now.

I cup my head in that curious way on the couch, fingertips surrounding my ear, palm as far away as a palm can be in such a position, my weight on the back of my hand and my wrist against the cushion. Elisa talks about what she's reading. I look at her lips.

Widener's reading room, Havi Carel's "Living in the Present: Illness, Phenomenology, and Well-Being."

Scuffs and echoes, the heavy latch of fire doors.

Carel, a British theorist and cancer survivor, on the experience of being ill:

> Meaning structures are . . . destabilized and in extreme cases the overall coherence of one's life is destroyed. Illness radically disrupts the fundamental sense of embodied normalcy in which one's existence is rooted.

A girl who I suspect for an international student approaches my corner (I used to teach international students and pride myself on spotting them from small fashion choices, the facial muscles formed from articulating different sorts of words; of course, I could be wrong). She pulls two easy chairs together to make a standing desk of the chairbacks.

I return to my book but now I can feel her eyes on my . . . feet. I had slipped off my shoes an hour ago and she's noticed. I presume she's scandalized but I misjudged: fixing her gaze at her computer, she slips her own shoes off, discretely, and toes them beneath a chair. Barefoot neighbors, we study quietly into the night.

I suspected Melissa would age well and she's proved me right. It's been fifteen years since she moved to Brooklyn but she looks only five years older. I remember her talking about aging when we were young, saying, "Extra pounds just appear in your twenties. Why? They just appear?" I hadn't noticed.

Café Algiers. My eyes still loved to trace the iron railing of the mezzanine and the clusters of hexagonal tables with their inlays of mother of pearl. But the place was in disarray tonight—the coffee came cold, the bathrooms hadn't been cleaned, there wasn't any wine left. "We've run out. We're closing in a week, for good." The building was sold, rents in Harvard Square deep in the decades-long process of firing up like a satellite launch, inviting only great criminals and the children of great criminals to make homes there.

I hadn't planned to meet Melissa; she just happened to be at Algiers with our friend Sarah. I was changed but she didn't seem much changed. For the moment, Algiers held itself in place. Melissa ran out to buy a few bottles of wine and we opened them at the table—a kind of impromptu goodbye party.

We toasted hello. Sarah and Melissa knew about my ears—they'd read something I'd written online about going deaf. Two glasses in, Melissa fixed her eyes on the top of my head. "Your hair . . ." she said, trailed off.

"Yeah, there's less of it."

She chided me. "I was going to say it was blonder."

She still wrote poetry, still lived in Brooklyn with her medievalist partner. Were things between them going well?

"Elisa," she said, leveling me with her eyes, "is a special woman. You be grateful you have that woman. You be good to her."

Why had she said it like a warning? But of course I understood: back in my twenties I was raffish. I was a joke rake—the shirt half-unbuttoned and the wine in my hand, louche. I played it for laughs. It went with the poetry. Fifteen years later I was deaf and I was married and I felt older than forty. I regarded the loucheness as buried, because it was. I'd experienced a revolution of the self when I became involved with Elisa, and then a second, of a very different sort, when my ears went bad. A third, now, learning to live in the world again, to live deaf and unsure of what might come next.

I grew tired easily; I drank only white wine as a policy, rarely more than two glasses. I strained to hear Melissa's voice. But . . . because Melissa had barely seen me these fifteen years, it was as if I still cut the same figure, the aging libertine. Through Melissa's eyes, that libertine was still alive. He was still me.

Time seemed to hiccup. After years of poisonous self-absorption, poisonous because self-loathing was such a part of it, I'd been turning my gaze outward for a time, trying to escape what Iris Murdoch called the "fat relentless ego." Yes, that was still the plan, to try and make myself useful. But this time in Boston had been useful. My past, such as it was, still belonged to me. And it wasn't alive in me alone.

Elisa was asleep. I lay awake next to her, powerful headphones in place, trying to hear Beethoven's String Quartet no. 14, the first movement, the softest of the movements (he loves to start soft). The strings pass to each other the sound of reaching, like a collection of dancers reaching up, failing, new hands reaching up.

But I couldn't hear Beethoven that night because I hear too much like him. I'd been thinking about him as I read about Swift: both grew irritable as they aged, paranoid, retentive. Earlier that day at the Widener, on a whim, I'd pulled Beethoven's letters from the shelf:

... my ears continue to hum and buzz day and night. I must confess that I lead a miserable life. For almost two years I have ceased to attend any social functions, just because I find it impossible to say to people: I am deaf ...

I get out of bed and walk through the house in the dark. As a child I was afraid of dark houses. Now I'm more afraid of my own body—I'm the haunted house. Dark trees in dark windows, dark green in the light from the streetlight. Even at night I want to stare at them. I'd forgotten that. For too long my life had been free of a tether to something oracular, something that, through a trick of the mind, seemed to network me into the secrets of nature, seemed to involve me.

I'm not a fool—I know I haven't been far from the mystery, but I haven't been able to see it, haven't been able to experience the extramundanity of what was happening to my own body as anything but pain.

As I moved through the apartment the hollow punch of drumming came in through the windows. We'd left them open.

My hearing aids were still in the bedroom, still in their case. I was glad, because with the aids on I couldn't detect the directionality of sound. Without them I knew what window to move toward, where to look. There, outside: a fenced backyard and weathered chairs and two dancers in a style I'd never seen. It was courtly how they moved, dancing rhythmically toward one another and then back to the sound of the two seated, cheering drummers. The drummers were men and the dancers were women; they were young, or they moved like they were young.

I watched them for what felt like too long—I was spying on neighbors and the neighbors weren't even mine. But I couldn't stop watching them. In memory, they wore regalia, wigs and silks, sashes you'd wear in the 1690s to meet the king. But they must have worn street clothes. And it must have been late, maybe 11 p.m.

When we left town, I wanted to go across the street and tell them thank you. But you can't say that to strangers, especially in Boston.

The Hundred Oceans of Jonathan Swift

Jonathan Swift saw what dying must be like. He watched an apple spin out of his hand while he held on to it one autumn day in 1689. He felt the ground list up as if he were falling through solid earth, or as though the earth were falling upward in a rush.

He couldn't breathe. That, more than the spinning, told him he was terribly sick. The world kept moving, but in an ugly way, as though he might slide off its face. The picture he saw—the garden he'd been walking through—reeled. He threw up onto the paving stones and the act centered him. His body was rejecting the sickness. He'd been gorging himself on sweet yellow apples and gluttony was a sin. Worse: it was foolish.

He groped his way out of the garden toward the house, but his hands were reaching out for purchase that wasn't there, and he fell on his knees and then his palms, bruising them. His employer would be furious; if he didn't die he'd be fired. He couldn't breathe. There was nothing to do now but shout and he did. When he felt the gardener's arm around him, he clutched the man's hand as if it were a raft.

Swift survived that attack, but it was weeks before he felt like himself. And he never stopped dreading another. Turning corners, shifting his head, he'd see the world tilt away from him. Sometimes it was all he could manage to stumble down the street back home, to whatever room he was renting, or into a church to find a pew. Within two years, his ears had started to lose not just their balance, but their hearing too.

I'm making some guesses, based on my own experiences—I couldn't breathe during my first attack, I reached for something to grab on to. But I'm making fewer guesses than you might imagine. I know Swift was in an orchard when the deafness hit, and I know he was eating apples when he first felt things spinning, "a hundred golden pippins at a time, at Richmond." He wrote volumes of letters about the minutia of his life, and he talked about his illness often. We don't have the letters from his years in the employ of William Temple, but we know that Temple had a Dutch-style garden (cobblestones, silence, fruiting trees in ordered rows) and that Swift—when he wasn't taking the old man's dictation—lingered there to read and munch on sweets.

Swift's mother was English, but her son was born and lived most of his life in Ireland, to his horror. Dublin in

1667 wasn't a charming park-strewn land of pubs and bookshops; it was an imperial backwater, and Swift, like a kind of Ovid born into exile, pined for the home he felt had been denied him. The best his mother could do was to land him a job in England with the most influential person she knew: a retired diplomat, William Temple, garden lover and amateur scholar who fancied himself an English Montaigne. Swift sailed across the Irish Sea, lived and worked in several of Temple's estates, and was eventually rewarded for his labor with the prestigious but shabby duty of editing the old man's collected works.

Among his responsibilities as Temple's companion and amanuensis was the tutoring of Esther Johnson, a young girl of the household, likely Temple's illegitimate daughter. Along with free run of Temple's library and plenty of time for reading, the company of Esther Johnson—Swift called her Stella—became his prime joy.

Time, at first, was good to Swift and Stella. The precocious girl he met at Temple's soon matured, at least in Swift's telling, into the sharpest and wittiest person in any room. She was patient with the slow but not the presumptuous. As Swift wrote after her death, "A rude or conceited coxcomb passed his time very ill, upon the least breach of respect; for in such a case she had no mercy." They had that in common. Both were black haired and striking; Swift was shorter than the ideal of his era and Stella was plumper. She wished he didn't flirt with other women, and he wished she worked harder at her French. She read his manuscripts with brutal honesty. Like Swift, she cared nothing for the fripperies of

fashion. He enjoyed the company of clever women, she
of clever men.

They got on swimmingly when they were young, but
it wasn't until later—when Stella was grown and Swift es-
tablished in Ireland—that she crossed the Irish Sea. They
may or may not have secretly married (why a secret? No one
knows). Once Swift left the employ of William Temple, he
and Stella never shared a house again, though she lived
nearby to the end. It was a strange arrangement that seemed
strange at the time. Most of what we know of their relationship we've learned from Swift's letters to Stella. There
he told her of nearly everyone he saw and nearly everywhere
he went in London. When he wrote to her, he called her
PPT (poor, pretty thing) or MD (my dear). He mentioned
his episodes of vertigo ("this morning, sitting in my bed, I
had a fit of giddiness"), but assured her he was all right; he'd
take care of himself, "for fear little MD should be angry."

Stella spent the rest of her life in Dublin, looking after some of Swift's poorer parishioners and fending off
intruders with a pistol. He praised her in verse, repeatedly, for sticking by him through his bouts of sickness,
even as they grew in frequency and rendered him all but
useless when they struck.

> When on my sickly couch I lay
> Impatient both of night and day,
> Lamenting in unmanly strains,
> Call'd every power to ease my pains;
> Then Stella ran to my relief
> With cheerful face and inward grief . . .

Was she ever impatient with him? Did she tire of such an unpredictable responsibility? How much should I read into the question from my own experience—my own relationships? There are probably answers I don't want to know. Poems like the above are a kind of thank-you, and inside of such a thank-you hides a wish.

Swift eventually came to blame the apples for his ailment, as did his doctors. Over a hundred years later, William Wilde, Oscar's father and a bigwig Dublin physician, thought Swift probably diagnosed himself just right. It *had* to be the apples. In *The Closing Years of Dean Swift's Life,* Wilde writes of the affliction, which he called "blood to the head":

> Overloading the stomach in the manner described, and catching cold by sitting on a damp, exposed seat, were very apt to produce both these complaints,—neither of which, when once established, was likely to be easily removed from a system so nervous, and with a temper so irritable, and a mind so excessively active, as that of Swift's.

Far from placing blame on Swift for his own condition—a habit we're hardly free from now—Wilde was racing to Swift's rescue, tamping down rumors of syphilis. Although there were doctors who connected vertigo and deafness in Swift's day, and although deafness was

obviously to do with the ear, vertigo was more mysterious. Even now, dizziness can spring from any number
of causes, and the doctors and biographers who poked
around Swift's bones and letters pinned what he called
his "giddiness" anywhere they could. The word *Ménière's*
was nothing but the name of a commercial family somewhere in France.

One Thomas Beddoes, in *Hygëia: or Essays Moral
and Medical,* grew to suspect that Swift was syphilitic.
Seven years later, William Makepeace Thackeray blamed
the pippins again. Dr. Samuel Johnson (not that kind of
doctor) assumed like a lot of people did that the mental deterioration of Swift's later years was entirely to
do with the disease driving him insane; he didn't blame
fruit, though. "The origin of diseases is commonly obscure," he wrote. "Almost every boy eats as much fruit as
he can get, without any great inconvenience." In 1908,
a Philadelphia ophthalmologist assumed he was settling
the matter for good by naming as culprit a very advanced
but not entirely uncommon form of eye strain.

In Dublin, a rumor still persists that Swift died confined
to a lunatic asylum. This would have been strange, since
the first such institution in Dublin was founded only after
Swift died and with money he'd specifically left to found
it. But the idea of such a clear mind totally shattered is too
romantic to abandon. William Butler Yeats wrote a play in
the 1930s that hinges on the diagnosis of Swift's vertigo
and his lunacy, *Words upon the Window Pane.*

Yeats dramatizes a séance in which Swift and Stella
come to life again, along with the lovesick Vanessa,

objcct—perhaps rightfully—of Stella's jealousy. Vanessa, in the play, wants two things: children with Swift and an end to Swift's relationship with Stella. "If you and she are not married," Vanessa asks, "why should we not marry like other men and women?"

Swift, in his answer, evokes the apples in Sheen:

I have something in my blood that no child must inherit. I have constant attacks of dizziness; I pretend they come from a surfeit of fruit when I was a child. I had them in London . . . There was a great doctor there, Dr. Arbuthnot; I told him of those attacks of dizziness, I told him of worse things. It was he who explained. There's a line of Dryden's . . .

Vanessa catches his meaning instantly. "O, I know— 'great wits are sure to madness near allied.' If you had children, Jonathan, my blood would make them healthy."

Over the half decade it took to write *Gulliver's Travels*, Swift confessed to a friend: "I used to be free of these Fits in a fortnight but now the Disease I fear is deeper rooted." He dreaded attacks of the deafness, the vertigo, the roar, for "when it is on me, I have neither spirits to write, or read, or think, or eat." He drank. (He bragged to his friend Alexander Pope, "I can bear a pint better than you can a spoonful.") Some doctors thought drinking was the cause, and others prescribed it. Some doctors prescribed pills to make him vomit, though the disease did that anyway. At various points he took handfuls of pills every day along with spa waters, aloes, Middle Eastern herbs, nutmeg presses, caustics, mercury, castor oil, lavender drops, antispasmodics, garlic drizzled in honey then inserted in the ear, and he probably rubbed his ears with phosphorous oil too (made from an apothecary's piss—Dr. Cockburn prescribed it and alchemist Godfrey of Southampton supplied the raw material and the magic).

Every symptom of this mystery sickness—down to the anxiousness and the way it forced his friends to shout—appears in *Gulliver's Travels*, between the end of Gulliver's adventure among the giants and his travels around the floating island. By the end of part two of the book, our doughty traveler has been given a dollhouse to live in (he calls it his "box") by the adolescent giantess Glumdalclitch. Alas, the box is snatched up by a giant eagle. Of the jolt when the ground falls out from under him, Gulliver writes, "I found myself suddenly awakened with a violent Pull upon the Ring which was fastened at the top of my Box, for the Conveniency of Carriage. I felt my box raised very high in the Air, and then borne forward with prodigious Speed." He calls out as loud as he can, but all he can hear is "a Noise just over my Head like a clapping of Wings." He "then began to perceive the woeful Condition I was in." Like nearly everything in the book, the ride is played for laughs:

In a little time I observed the noise and flutter of Wings to increase very fast, and my Box was tossed up and down like a Signpost in a windy Day. I heard several Bangs or Buffets, as I thought, given to the Eagle (for such I am certain it must have been that held the Ring of my Box in his Beak) and then all on a sudden felt myself falling perpendicularly down for above a Minute, but with such incredible Swiftness that I almost lost my Breath. My Fall was stopped by a terrible Squash, that sounded louder to my Ears than the Cataract of *Niagara*.

This is obviously delightful, but it's not possible for a person who suffers from chronic vertigo to read the passage above and not recognize the rising noise, the feeling of being tossed in the wind or falling through the air, and the breath that disappears from the narrator's lungs. (I'd be shocked if he was unconscious of that pun on his own name too—Jonathan was as conscious of being a Swift as Shakespeare was of being a Will.)

I think the roar of Niagara is the giveaway. Swift always used metaphors of water to describe the sounds in his ears to friends: "a hundred oceans" or "the Noise of seven Watermills in my Ears." Watermills because they were the closest the eighteenth century got to the noise of engines (they are, essentially, giant engines). When Jonathan Swift was in his sixties, a fellow sufferer wrote to her doctor in Paris: "It is not the deafness which hampers me. I can put up with that, it is the noise of mills, of drums, above all at night, increase to the point that I cannot sleep, and the banging that rings from one ear to the other."

Eventually Gulliver is rescued by a passing ship full of people of his own size and shape. The captain of the ship that saves him from the sea "wondered at one thing very much, which was to hear me speak so loud, asking me whether the King or Queen of that Country were thick of Hearing." He goes on to beautifully describe what it is like to live with the sort of low-frequency hearing loss his condition left him with: "When I spoke in that Country, it was like a Man talking in the Street to another looking out from the Top of a Steeple."

Is life a comedy or a tragedy? I'll ask that another way: is time cyclical or unidirectional? Whichever you answer, don't be so sure. Progressive illness puts a finger on the scale. But with Ménière's disease—at least some species of what we now call Ménière's—there exists a long period of indeterminacy, of transient episodes and strange noises that overwhelm and then vanish in cycles. A period when we still have the heart to try nutmeg presses, caustics, phosphorous (the period when, if we live in Colorado, friends recommend CBD oil, or craniosacral massage, or microdosing).

Then the disease grows "deeper rooted."

If life is unidirectional, if the story only has one ending, you'll want to look for a story within the story. You'll look for a frame within the frame.

. . .

To keep finding answers, change the questions.

Swift was a decade into the world of dizziness when Antonio Valsalva first identified the tiny parts of the inner ear. (We know this name today from the "Valsalva maneuver": pinch your nose and blow out your cheeks— your ears pop). Working at the University of Bologna, Valsalva rushed to dissect fresh corpses, in mind of how the delicate membranes of the ear begin to deteriorate mere seconds after death. There, with the aid of a microscope, Valsalva separated the parts of the ear to isolate the little tuning forks of bone that pick up sounds from our ear drums and pass them along to the vestibule and cochlea.

If we can agree the organs of the ear resemble a snail, then it makes sense to say the vestibular tubes are that snail's antennae and the cochlea is its coil. Corpses with damaged cochlea often had little to no hearing in life, so anatomists understood almost instantly that the cochlea must be where sound resonates, and where it's transformed into something the mind can read. But how?

Today we know the cochlea's coils are grown full with cilia hairs: little flagella that vibrate in time with the bones where the outer sounds resonate. Your eardrum carries the sound to the bones, the bones to the hair cells of the cochlea, and nerves at the end of those cells to the brain. Place your finger just above the hole in your ear (not *in* the hole, just above it); if you were to push that finger straight through, past the ear drum and bones and the cochlea to your brain, you would follow the path of that cranial nerve for a while, before it bends down into the medulla, the lizard stem, to be distributed to the periphery.

Swift was cold in the ground, his skeleton turning black, when French physiologist Jean Pierre Flourens had the first inkling that the semicircular canals were used for something other than hearing. Flourens tortured pigeons for his experiments, and in the course of several sessions discovered the birds become disoriented when the semicircular canals (the snail's antennae) were snipped. The sabotaged animals would fall forward, or back, or spin in circles. Flourens didn't know why this was happening—maybe the canals controlled some kind of movement?

By 1835, St. Patrick's Cathedral in Dublin had flooded so much the catacombs beneath it had to be cleaned and fitted with new supports. In the course of the swabbing-out, Jonathan Swift was dug up and his skull taken out for examination. Thanks partially to prominent marks left by an enlarged vein, our friend William Wilde lamented Swift wasn't alive to be trepanned. Wilde carried the skull around with him on the Dublin social circuit for weeks, explaining how a simple crack by an awl, right *there*, could have fixed Swift's deafness and dizziness in a stroke. Also prescribed for the same disease: leeches to the buttocks.

. . .

Born in 1799, Prosper Menière lived a happier life than Swift. Part of that happiness was simple disposition: Menière was also denied the jobs he felt he deserved, but he took defeat philosophically. Menière was existentially lucky too, born to moneyed parents who helped him to ensure that both his medical and his literary talents would be rewarded well into middle age. As a young man, Menière worked as a trauma surgeon during the riots of 1830 and later wrote a successful book about it. He studied Latin poetry and lectured on orchids. He loved the sound of Italian opera and took in shows every chance he got.

When Menière was appointed physician-in-chief at France's National Institution for Deaf-Mutes in 1838, he arrived in a small hell. Deaf patients at the time were subject to cruel experiments: their ears were burned until they blistered, then scrubbed and burned again; the skull behind their ears was struck by hammers and electro cuted with shocks. One physician-sufferer went so far as to have a piece of cloth strung straight through his neck in a last-ditch attempt to hear once more (oozing puss from the infection, so the theory went, would carry the disease away from the head when it drained). Many of these creepy experiments were performed on unwilling children, some of whom screamed and thrashed so much they couldn't be sufficiently restrained. They were the lucky ones—others died.

Menière, appalled, put a stop to the barbarity and attempted to learn what he could from the corpses of residents who'd died and from objective observation of the living. In 1861 he presented the result of twenty years of study establishing the definitive connection between hearing loss and vertigo as two aspects of the same condition. To make his argument to the academy he relied on two key cases. In the first, a young man with roaring in the ears and unstable hearing, who would suddenly appear stricken, without any obvious cause:

> A condition of indescribable distress drained his strength; his face pale and bathed with sweat proclaimed approaching collapse . . . lying on his back he could not open his eyes without seeing the objects around him whirling in space; the slightest movement of the head increased the vertigo and nausea; vomiting started again as soon as the patient tried to change his position.

I imagine Swift would have looked like this at his worst, though various fits hit him differently. He could walk at times, if unsteadily. "I walk like a drunken Man," he told Revrand Thomas Sheridan in 1727, when he was "deafer than ever you knew me." Other sufferers report a sensation of aura before the spells strike, although "aura" might mean almost anything—flashing lights, a feeling of profound unease, an eerie tone. Some patients report discrete episodes of vertigo; for others, months filled wholly up with them. A year after that letter to Sheridan, Swift wrote of an eight-month period during which he "had at least half a dozen returns of my giddiness and

deafness, which lasted me about three weeks a piece."
Meaning he was sick more often than not, for over half
a year. This happens to patients with Ménière's disease; it
happened to me.

It rained cold on the January Ménière presented his famous lecture to France's Imperial Academy of Medicine.
Ménière, to his chagrin, was not an academy member,
so he couldn't be counted on to draw a crowd. He didn't.
And the rain didn't help. He delivered his talk to a few
half-bored attendees and then shuffled off to revise it for
publication.

Contrast this with the commotion at the academy
in the week that followed, when the celebrated internist Armand Trousseau took a running kick at Wilde's
beloved cerebral congestion. Trousseau understood
the movement of blood through the brain (it was he
who coined the term "aphasia"), and he maintained
that cerebral congestion was diagnosed far too often.
Citing Ménière's paper of the week before, he urged
the academy members in attendance to keep more
open minds and rely on more direct research, rather
than trust in the received wisdom that had steered
them wrong in the past.

A dozen years later in Vienna, a pair of friends
named Josef Breuer and Ernst Mach conducted several
experiments—on the living and the dead—to develop
a convincing, if patchy, theory of how the vestibular

canals actually functioned, and what happened inside those canals.

Breuer, a family physician to the cream of Vienna, hypothesized that the fluid inside the labyrinth of the ear—a positively ionized potassium substance called endolymph—washed up against the inside of the vestibular canals, triggering receptors, as though the inside of the labyrinth were a half-filled snow globe with sensors on the inside of the dome; when the dome was turned, those sensors would light up on contact with the liquid. The "snow" in this analogy are otoliths, tiny calcium stones that settle on the base of the labyrinth when we're upright, then become unbalanced when our position changes. But German physicist Ernst Mach wasn't sure about any of it. He thought the fluid didn't have much at all to do with sensing motion in the ears.

If you're traveling at 343 meters per second, then you're traveling at the speed of sound: Mach 1. Ernst Mach wasn't going nearly that fast on the railway train that inspired his dissent, but that train was going fast enough that when it hit a sharp curve the scenery appeared to tilt away from Mach at a strange angle. The train wasn't tilting—the world was. Why? Mach theorized that pressure, not fluid, told our brains how to react to motion. To play around with the idea, he built a pressure sensor in a model vestibule, but the results of his experiment were inconclusive.

Whether the endolymph lapped the insides of those narrow tubes or pressure conducted a charge to the hair cells, whatever happened inside the canals seemed crucial. And for a while it looked as though Menière had reached that conclusion first. In his paper from 1861, Menière described an autopsy of a young girl who'd experienced vertigo and hearing loss. And in the course of that surgery he discovered, in Robert Baloh's paraphrase, "red plastic material, a bloody exudate, filling the semicircular canals but not the cochlea." This, then, was proof that hemorrhage in the canals could serve as sole cause of vertigo. It was proof of how the disease *worked*.

Except that it wasn't true. In his own notes from 1848, thirteen years before he delivered his famous paper, Menière described the same case—the girl, the symptoms, the ear—but in those notes he described the *entire ear* as filled with fluid: a far larger hemorrhage than the one he'd implied in his paper.

Menière's theory was revolutionary, yes, but his sloppy methodology did damage. As late as 1950, physicians still expected to trace vertigo caused by Menière's disease to a hemorrhage of the canals, when hemorrhage might, after all, have nothing to do with it. (The girl from 1848 probably suffered from leukemia, and that was probably what killed her.)

Two of those physicians who found themselves misled were the Anglo-Indian otologist Charles Hallpike and the Australian surgeon Hugh Cairns. Hallpike was an expert on the ear thanks to long evenings and weekends above the dissection table, and Cairns knew the vestibule from snipping it. Cutting the vestibular nerve, or one of the canals that attach to it, was a treatment approved for life-altering attacks. It sometimes offered a measure of relief, but it was full of risk: patients routinely died on the table from brain infections or lost at least some of the hearing that remained.

Thanks to the samples of ears Cairns collected in the mid-1930s, he and Hallpike were able to theorize that Ménière's disease was characterized by a swelling throughout the membranes, probably caused by excess of endolymph. Thus, "endolymphatic hydrops" became associated with Ménière's disease, to the extent that "idiopathic endolymphatic hydrops" is now an official, medically accepted synonym for the disease.

As far as treatment was concerned, there Cairns and Hallpike were at a loss, as physicians had been before them and physicians would be after. In coming years, novel remedies would fall in and out of practice when they proved indistinguishable from placebo effects. One treatment in particular—a shunt to regulate the flow of endolymph between several parts of the ear—is still sometimes in use today, but there's nothing except for anecdotal evidence to show that it works. No doctor has ever recommended it to me. Postmortem examinations find the shunts pushed aside or occluded: they work only for a few days, a few hours.

Progress on the further definition and treatment of the condition has been, as one leading researcher puts it, "frustratingly slow." Dr. Carol Foster, former director of the Balance Laboratory at University of Colorado

Hospital, laments in a paper that a basic confusion in what did or didn't count as strict Ménière's meant in practice that "many articles purporting to treat Ménière's disease over the past 75 years have included patients with unrelated disorders." This is why people tell me they've been diagnosed with Ménière's because they felt a little dizzy, once, years ago.

As late as 1994, the American Academy of Otolaryngology – Head and Neck Surgery didn't have a definition of the syndrome narrow enough to keep disparate researchers on the same page about what disease they were researching. Questions remain. The academy's definition insists that "hearing loss is often intermittent, occurring mainly at the time of the attacks of vertigo," but Swift's hearing fluctuated at entirely different times than his vertigo struck. My own hearing never stops rising and falling, but vertigo comes and goes, sometimes going away for a long time. Why?

"Every case is unique," Foster told me in her examination room. "Swelling of the inner ear isn't even the significant predictor that we thought it was. Because we've done dissections of people who had no symptoms, but they did have that swelling. So there's something else at play."

She leaned forward in her chair. "It's a terrible disease." She has it too.

. . .

In Book IV of *Gulliver's Travels*, poor longsuffering Lemuel is once again swept off by a storm, only to land on an island full of crazy primates and horses that talk. *Yahoos* are what the horses call the ape things, and particularly frightening is the reveal of what the Yahoos really are.

Those Yahoos who taunt Gulliver and fling excreta in one another's faces, who reek and jibber and ugly themselves by fighting and biting are, horribly, Gulliver's fellow human beings, albeit preserved in a state of nature.

The other species on the island, Houyhnhnms, who herd and govern these Yahoos (as well as such miserable creatures can be governed) are handsome and hyper-rational masters. Identical in physiognomy to the horses of Europe, the Houyhnhnms adopt Gulliver and accord him the respect due to his unusual nature—he's the first example they've seen of a Yahoo with the remotest sense of reason, or of right and wrong.

Because the equine Houyhnhnms live so measured and sensible an existence, disease is virtually unknown to them. It is thus with some sense of wonder they come to understand Gulliver's description of what contemporary doctors of medicine in Europe are and what they do. The primary theory of disease in the land he's from, he explains, is that too much of some substance collects in the blood and must be purged out one way or another. The weird medicines Swift himself was prescribed—and that some sufferers of Ménière's are still prescribed—come in for especial condemnation. Doctors in Europe, Gulliver explains, still went in for

the ancient theory that a surplus of one sort of fluid or
spirit causes all disease:

> ... whence they conclude, that a great *Evacuation*
> of the Body is necessary, either through the natu-
> ral Passage, or upwards at the Mouth. Their next
> Business is, from Herbs, Minerals, Gums, Oils,
> Shells, Salts, Juices, Seaweed, Excrements, Barks
> of Trees, Serpents, Toads, Frogs, Spiders, Dead
> Men's Flesh and Bones, Birds, Beasts, and Fishes,
> to form a Composition for Smell and Taste the
> most abominable, nauseous and detestable, they
> can possibly contrive, which the Stomach imme-
> diately rejects with loathing; and this they call
> a *Vomit*; or else from the same Storehouse, with
> some other poisonous Additions, they command
> us to take in at the Orifice *above* or *below* (just as
> the Physician then happens to be disposed).

Swift undoubtedly felt there was an element of whim
to the prescriptions he was given, and he was undoubtedly right. But then he was accustomed to living by the
whims of others: the nursemaid who decided, for whatever reason, to kidnap him to England for three years
when he was a child, the patron who might have introduced the young man to society but declined, the politicians who never awarded Swift the bishopric he craved,
and the doctors who seemed to be pulling their cures
from a hat.

Dizziness is distinct from vertigo proper: the former implies mere unsteadiness, while the latter makes
a room-spinning nightmare. But Swift had both, one
blending into the other, increasing as he aged. "It would
be difficult," Leo Damrosch concludes in his excellent
biography from 2013, "to exaggerate the lifelong burden
this became."

By the 1720s, we find Swift writing to his friend
Knightley Chetwode:

> I have been these five weeks and still continue so
> disordered with a Noise in my Ears and Deafness
> that I am utterly unqualifyed for all Conversation
> or thinking. . . . I never stir out, or suffer any to see
> me but Trebbles and countertennors, and those as
> seldom as possible.

Trebles and countertenors because for whatever
still-uncertain reason, Ménière's disease is characterized
by low-decibel loss that eventually flattens into complete
loss—meaning men's voices go first, while women's persist a while longer, though not forever. Eventually, though
you can probably still hear some sound, you can't make
sense of human speech. The jokes and the stories and the
good advice of the people around you are indistinguishable from babble, from what a Yahoo says.

Swift didn't have technology to come to his aid, but
technology can only do so much. I pop in my Widex
Dreams first thing when I wake up, and those aids communicate real sound by pixelating and then reconstructing

it. The once-rich piano becomes a toy piano, heard as though on a radio through a radio. When the notes begin to fall on top of one another, they blend and muddy. It's possible to pick up the thread, but it comes through memory, not the sound around me. These days I still dance at weddings, but after a few bars of each new song I have to lean in to ask my wife what it is. "Billie Jean" (which I used to jog to along the shore) is indistinguishable from static unless I know it's "Billie Jean"—then I can follow the beats, and the rhythm falls into place.

Helen Keller is credited with observing that "blindness separates people from things; deafness separates people from people." Like me, Swift worried about this kind of thing constantly, and once his eyes began to fail he gave in to dejection. Stella died during the enthusiasm over *Gulliver's Travels,* and Swift was too ill to go to her funeral. That night, instead of walking down the street to the churchyard, he lay in his bed, too sick to move. Funeral music came faintly through the deanery's windows, but the rushlights in the room wouldn't quit jerking back and forth, and he had to focus on one of them and keep his attention there all night to avoid his mind drifting to darker corners, corners where he was too often at home.

He traveled to England to see his old friends, but he felt deafer than he'd expected; arriving, he refused their company. Frustrated with passing notes back and forth, certain this was an irritation to Alexander Pope and the others, he spent his time making poems from his dejection.

Deaf, giddy, odious to my friends,
Now all my consolation ends;
No more I hear my church's bell
Than if it rang out for my knell;

Pope had a weak voice to boot, unlike the long-serv-
ing staff at Swift's deanery who could bawl into his ears,
or his friend Mrs. Worrall, "a chearfull woman with a
clear voice." He didn't inflict himself on others, certain
he was "a worthless companion."

Swift fled Pope's country house in England and there-
after never left Ireland, becoming increasingly isolated
and increasingly bitter. ("The giddiness I was subject to,
instead of coming seldom, and violent, now constantly
attends me, more or less, tho in a more peaceable Manner,
yet such as will not qualify me to live among the young
and healthy.")

As he lamented to Charles Ford:

You healthy People cannot judge of the Sickly.
Since I had yʳ last of Mar. 10ᵗʰ I have not been able
to write; and three Days ago having invited sever-
all Gentlemen to dinner, I was so attacked with a
fitt of Giddyness for 5 Hours . . . I lay miserable
on my Bed. Your friendly Expostulations force me
upon this old Woman's Talk, but I can bring all my
few Friends to witness that you have heard more
of it, than ever I troubled them with.

One of Swift's friends, a quietly awful person named Mary Delany, wrote of him: "He talks a great deal and does not require many answers."

He couldn't hear her.

Before we can treat Ménière's disease effectively, we have to figure out what causes it. Swift's doctors believed—based on little but superstition—that an excess of vital fluids was to blame. By the end of the twentieth century most physicians and researchers were convinced that fluid was endolymph.

So is hydrops—swelling caused by an excess of endolymph—the final answer? Maybe yes and maybe no; maybe *yes, but.* A 2005 paper by Merchant et al. in *Otology & Neurotolgy*, the journal of the American Otological Society, described a study on the remains of more than a hundred cadavers that discovered plenty of cases of hydrops—but it wasn't that simple. Only fifty-one of seventy-nine patients with swollen inner ears ever reported anything like Ménière's symptoms in life—meaning hydrops, however common, could not be "directly responsible" for their trouble. If hydrops is synonymous with Ménière's, a finding like this should be impossible.

There is research being done, but considering how damaging the condition can be, there's a good deal less research than one might expect. I have alerts set up to read new material in every way I can, and I periodically scroll PubMed for new articles and NIH grant recipients to see who's putting out calls. Still, more than 300 years after Valsalva parsed the ear, and 350 after Swift was born in Dublin, research hasn't turned up any golden bullets, or even a clear idea of how to find one.

Foster thinks the missing mechanism may be circulatory. Along with her neurosurgical colleague Dr. Robert Breeze, Foster is researching whether a predisposition to vascular disease is what makes existing cases of hydrops dangerous, triggering attacks. If her theory is correct, Ménière's may be related to migraines, and Ménière's sufferers may be at higher risk of atherosclerosis. Could Swift's Ménière's be connected, however tenuously, to the strokes that killed him? Might Dr. William Mackenzie of Glasgow, in a letter of 1846, be accidentally correct when he concludes it was the roaring and the spinning in both ears that caused the already irascible Swift to lose his senses entirely and fall "furiously insane"?

Maybe. But what this means in practice is hard to say. Foster prescribes vasodilators, low-dose aspirin, omega-3s, and magnesium supplements (to balance the calcium channels that, according to her theory, may be destroying the ear). Diuretics are still standard in the United States, although study after study concludes they produce no measurable effect. In the United Kingdom, the standard treatment is betahistine, though again, the vast majority of controlled studies show little benefit. I stopped taking diuretics in 2019, and if anything, my ears are better without them.

One of the reasons learning more has been so

difficult is that the inner ear is tricky to access while the patient is still alive. The temporal bone of the ear is incredibly hard and thick, and that little snail in your ear is incredibly small—on the scale of a pencil eraser—but with an elaborately complex structure and chemical balance. Any intrusive surgery is bound to damage it—just the shock from cutting through the bone could break it irreparably.

Swift didn't have the sort of mind that would turn to suicide, but by 1736 he was in a bad enough state to complain to Pope that "years and Infirmatyes have quite broke me. I mean that odious continual disorder in my Head. I neither re[a]d, nor write; nor remember, nor converse." He repeated his lament in letter after letter, telling Sheridan "a long Fit of Deafness, which still continues, hath unquali fied me for conversing, or thinking, or reading, or hearing; to all this is added an Apprehension of Giddiness, whereof I have frequently some frightful Touches." He couldn't leave his island, and then his town, and then his room.

He could walk until the end—he loved walking—but he "tottered" all the while, especially in the dark. This was probably oscillopsia.

On top of all this, Swift suffered a stroke, or something like it, in the years before the end, and it took his memory. Vascular trouble of some sort caused a bulging in his eye. The people who looked after him in his final years remember a man profoundly deaf and by then nearly blind, who couldn't recognize his old friends and muttered detached lines to no one like "I am what I am."

Gulliver's Travels, a bitterly misanthropic book, has long been considered appropriate for children. But perhaps those children aren't reading the original text, and I suspect most aren't. Abridged children's versions and children's films stick only to the first of the book's four sections: the adorable Lilliputians. Gulliver's tiny captors are objectively cute, at least at first; at least if you set aside how rapaciously homicidal they are toward their neighbors, the Blefuscudians.

But they do render Gulliver's comparatively enormous body disgusting, as a Lilliputian friend of the traveler confesses: "he could discover great Holes in my Skin, that the Stumps of my Beard were ten times stronger than the Bristles of a Boar, and my Complexion made up of several Colours altogether disagreeable."

Gulliver himself learns this firsthand when he washes ashore on Brobdingnag. The people there are giants, "as tall as an ordinary Spire-steeple." They smell very bad of course, but "after all, I found their natural Smell was much more supportable than when they used Perfumes, under which I immediately swooned away." Being large, their voices are thunderously loud, and their simple cries of astonishment "pierced my Ears like that of a Water-Mill."

So put off is Gulliver by the monstrous size of these otherwise comely creatures that he even finds it upsetting when "the handsomest among these Maids of Honour, a pleasant frolicsome Girl of sixteen, would sometimes set me astride upon one of her Nipples, with many other

Tricks, wherein the Reader will excuse me for not being over particular."

The giants, whatever their faults, at least have the gift of reason. Not so the Yahoos. According to the Houyhnhnms, and as verified by Gulliver firsthand, our brother and sister Yahoos gibber and slap one another, fight brutally over shiny stones, mate screechingly wherever they please, pimp for their pack leaders, loaf, fall into intoxication by sucking a strange root, and collapse into maladies of spleen.

> I did indeed observe, that the *Yahoos* were the only Animals in this Country subject to any Diseases; which however, were much fewer than Horses have among us, and contracted not by any ill Treatment they meet with, but by the Nastiness, and Greediness of that sordid Brute.

At bottom, *Gulliver's Travels* is a satire on the awfulness of human bodies, the paucity of our reason, the weaknesses in our appetites. Swift had his own grove of apples (like William Temple he was a cultivator, even getting nectarines to grow in Dublin in the open air). But his doctors convinced him that fruit was a poison to someone in his condition, and so he disciplined himself to avoid it. "I will be very Temperate," he writes in a letter, "and in the midst of Peaches, Figs, Nectarines, and Mulberries, I touch not a bit."

Did the way Swift's body turned against him help to make *Gulliver's Travels* the book it became? Of course, Gulliver is not Swift (Gulliver is a surgeon, a credulous soul, and he isn't Irish). And of course, the Houyhnhnms' question of "whether the *Yahoos* should be exterminated from the Face of the Earth" is intended—mostly—as a satire on the excesses of reason, rather than a cri de coeur.

It's easy to see from whence rumors of madness may have sprung. All his adult life, Swift lived with spinning and a roar in his head. Stella's death increased a preexisting tendency to tetchiness. When his memory grew less reliable, then disappeared, it was easy to assume that's where those disorders of the head had been leading him all along. Those rendered deaf, even now, are more prone to dementia (and if that deafness arises from a vascular source, as Ménière's might, those suffering from vertigo and tinnitus along with their deafness may be additionally at risk).

Swift was bitter and anxious all his life, whether because of inborn temperament or the way he was formed by the disease that pursued him is impossible to say. Both? If it's true that circumstance reveals character, it is equally true that circumstance becomes character. Like trees, we bend to the shape of the light that falls.

Walking with Edward Young and some friends outside of Dublin one evening, Swift is reported to have pointed at an elm whose topmost branches were decayed. "I shall be like that tree," he said, "I shall die at the top." In the course of a long and difficult and sometimes triumphant life, he did.

Other Lives

I was eighteen when I heard the expression "a former life" in a context that wasn't about reincarnation. My teacher at the time, Peggy Rambach, spoke it offhandedly in the course of running a class. I was a bad student there and all through college—truculent, convinced I knew more than my teachers, petty about it when I did. My mother recently joked that a life of teaching has been my penance for how I acted back then. She's probably right.

I don't remember much about class that day, but I do remember Peggy had been telling a story from her life. It would have been wry and to the point, because she was both of those things. What was the story? Regardless, she dismissed it. "Well, it doesn't matter. That was a former life."

Peggy's was a single class in four years full of them. If I ever think about her, it's for that one phrase. Walking home from class, I decided that Peggy was too young to use a phrase like that and mean it. It reeked of affectation.

How could a living woman of—what? Thirty-eight?—
have a former life? How could anyone? We have the one,
and we're always living it. Peggy was attempting to seem
worldly, and to undergraduates. How gruesome.

But it was no act. Years later I came across a book
she'd written about her marriage to a man who'd been
considered—back when I knew Peggy, and when she
was writing the book—a giant of American letters. He
wooed her, left his wife to be with her, then fractured his
spine in an auto accident, changing his life and, of course,
hers. They divorced. Now she was adjuncting in a basement in Boston. She was making her own way.

It couldn't have felt like the same life anymore.

I bought the book.

More steady, I work longer hours now. When I'm not
working I take long walks on Denver's sun-blurred
streets, and half the time I walk to Bardo Coffee House
on South Broadway. There's a room in the back that's
removed from the whine of the steamer—as I've learned
in recent years, hearing aids make such things twice as
loud. Its walls are lined with couches that may have been
new in the late '90s, and the lighting is supplied by table
lamps that cast a glow on a brick wall peeled of whatever
once obscured it.

Not long ago my old friend Tony met me for an afternoon coffee here when he passed through town. I hadn't
seen him since he moved to Miami two years back.

"You seem better than last time," he said. "I was really worried about you. Last time I saw you it kinda seemed like it was eating you up from the inside."

I didn't know how to take this, because the last thing he'd said to me, two years before, was "You should be all right. It doesn't look like it's eating you up inside."

At Bardo he asked me what had changed to make it seem either like I was better, or like I was handling things better. Not thinking before I spoke, I answered, "I've learned how to put on a better act."

He squinted at me, which is how Tony registers concern. Dramatic like me, he overplays emotion on his face, even when it's real.

"That's not true," I said. "Forget that I said that. I think the answer is I'm gradually forgetting how to be the person I used to be. I can't separate *me* from *it* anymore. Maybe that makes it easier?"

One of these answers is probably true, but I don't know which.

I miss teaching big classes so—unsure if I'll be up for it—I sign up to teach refugees at an old community college in Denver. It's a storytelling class, and I'll run it alongside a pair of photographers. I'm reassured by this. What I mishear, my coteachers can repeat for me. I miss days for vertigo, but somehow, I don't miss too many. The school isn't far from where I live; when I'm too dizzy to drive, I walk.

The idea of the class is to get the students to write a few lines about their life, then to put those lines up on signs around town; in this way, it is hoped, Denverites will come to understand their new neighbors, empathize with how deserving and, yes, nonthreatening refugees can be, especially with the election underway and dark emotions turning darker.

Everyone in the room is still learning English, albeit at different speeds. Although one of the women, a pastor, speaks with only the faintest trace of an accent, another, a former journalist from Sudan, can't seem to form even simple words in a way we can understand—she just shakes her head after one bad try, raises her wrist to her forehead, and squints, a gesture I think I understand, though I can't be sure.

Their experiences in the world are involvingly varied: one was a nurse in Colombia, another an orchid keeper in Vietnam. But as I prompt them with questions to write about, I feel repeatedly surprised by how alike their answers sound.

What do you miss from your past?

The warmth of home, the smell of grandmother's cooking.

What is life like in the present?

Confusing. Lonely.

What surprises you about Denver?

People sleeping on the streets. In my country they'd be with family.

When you picture your future, what do you hope?

Safe children. To feel at home. To live my dreams.

. . .

Imagining total deafness coming on isn't difficult, because I've felt it at odd moments: a battery failure in the
chips and magnets behind my ears, or when I unhook
them to sleep. Without my hearing aids in place, on a
bad day, I encounter a world where only the low-pitched
roar in my ear is real. I love Elisa's voice, but when I'm
completely deaf it'll attenuate too thin to reach me. The
voices I know from the phone will lose their silkiness,
vanishing the people behind them. They'll convert into
words on a screen.

I worry for my eyes. When they tire, the past becomes
an animal. Every slight rises. It's tiring to lean in and
watch lips, to concentrate without cease.

Now I get through days by understanding that,
when the worst happens, if it happens, when sound
disappears for good, or when the dizziness progresses,
such a thing will be another life. Not a posthumous life,
but something that changes me into a person I can't see
from here. I know how I react to loss, but I don't know
how he will.

"Where are you from?"
    "Turkey."
    "Was English your second language after Turkish?"
    "Oh, no, I'm not Turkish. I came there from Syria."
    "Oh, Jesus, what town?"

"Damascus," Sara says, unselfconsciously. She wears a pink hijab and her English is better than the English of, if not *most* Americans, lots of Americans.

"When did you leave Damascus?"

"Two years ago. We've been waiting in Istanbul, and traveling to Balikesir to do paperwork. I don't like that place. The minute you step into the city you can feel this sadness."

"You grew up in Damascus?"

"Yes, but I wasn't born there," she says. "I moved there when I was a little girl. We came there from Iraq."

Sara studied psychology in Syria, and she wants to do that in America too. It was a challenge, though, because Arabic is her first language. I ask her to teach me a few words and she laughs, embarrassed on my behalf. "You can't speak *any* Arabic at *all?*"

"Most Americans can't!"

"Don't they offer a class at school?"

I consider playfully shouting something about how I'm deaf and can hardly be blamed, but even that is no excuse. Millions of Arabic readers must be deaf.

My face is serious as I contemplate this; I know because Sara smiles to disarm me. Only once, in fact, in the course of our work, do I catch her unsmiling. It begins when I ask what surprised her about Denver when she moved here. She says the place's energy.

"I think this is a thing." She's already comfortable in idiom. "I have a strong extra sense—sixth sense—and I love that Denver is so empty. Crowded cities are too much for someone like me. Someone sensitive."

I ask Sara to photograph something in Denver that symbolizes her past. The next time we meet she shows me a picture of a blue sky, empty except for a few streaks of light where the sun halos a corner and blurs it.

"This is my past, because it represents the first time I saw the sky in Denver."

She's been here three months. What about something before that? What was Damascus like? I don't ask this idly: one of the reasons we're both here is to help the people of Denver to accept their fellow citizens. Presumably, knowing what Sara had to deal with in Syria would help them to welcome her more heartily.

"Most people in America don't know much about Damascus," I tell her, "me included. So maybe you could write a couple of paragraphs about what your life was like when you lived there?"

I have an ulterior motive, of course. Sara signed up for the class with the understanding her work would be shared with the public in town. She could take the class without sharing work, but the spirit of the class is one of openness.

Days later, she hands me a brief text describing the walk home from eighth grade at Al-Abaseyen Middle School, "sunny and bright, relaxed, excited and safe." She talks about the smells of jasmine trees, window shopping with her best friend Siliny, "laughing at the same silly jokes and talking about how we are going to be famous and successful at 22."

She tells me she's twenty-one now, so success may have to wait. "But we were just girls."

"Do you have any photos we could pair with the text?"

Precisely that moment is when she stops smiling. She takes out her cell phone and flips for a picture she wants to show me. "This is my grandmother's house."

It's tricky, at first, to make sense of what I'm looking at. A picture of a parking garage in what looks like a jungle; the sun beats overhead but vines nearly cover the building's face. Zooming in, I see it's not a garage but a city block—the vines are wires and the flowers exploded rebar. There's nothing there.

"My god, Sara. I'm so sorry. You took this?"

"My grandmother took the picture before she left for Turkey."

There are seven more students to work with this afternoon—we won't have the computer room for weeks after this. In half an hour class ends.

"I don't know what you think, but I feel like this picture would really help people understand what's happening there, Sara. Could we maybe talk about ways to include it?"

"I don't focus on that kind of thing." She's still not smiling. "I'm thinking only about good things."

I write these words six months later in Maine, in eight-degree weather. I've scored a room above an art gallery for the next few weeks. The gallery owns the room, and they're letting me stay here free. It's like I've pulled a con.

This evening, as I sit upstairs typing, I wonder again at how the experience of illness, and of working to adapt to it, has changed me, maybe out of recognition. As I type I sip coffee from a pink toucan mug—the beak is the handle—and get distracted by what's happening outside. The little machines are loud behind my ears and I can hear the wind work its way down an alley at twenty-five miles per hour.

I love this sound. I lived half my twenties in a Boston apartment that faced an alley, and the bay windows rattled once a week. That same howl sounds outside now. It's like a banshee against the glass. Somehow, the hearing aids aren't hurting it. Or my memory's filling the gaps.

The Boston building where I sat up listening to the wind as a kid burned to the ground when I moved out to Denver. The *Globe* ran front-page pictures. Forty people lost their homes. In the pictures, an alley-side window gapes with flames.

Tired of listening, I put on my hat and walk down Commercial Street. It's crowded with Christmas shoppers and a bicyclist passes me angrily—I hadn't heard him. The volume level on my hearing aids is set too softly for speech. Not wanting to impede another bicycle, I reach into my pocket to raise the volume with the remote fob I carry. "Testing," I say aloud, then, "Testing one, two, three." The woman passing on my left startles—who am I addressing? Why am I talking so loud? I've seen this happen a hundred times—libraries, airports—say "testing" aloud and incite those around with suspicion. I pull the fob from my pocket and thumb "+" to make the world louder still. "Testing."

I'm a man walking down a busy street saying the word *testing* at different volumes as he rummages in his pocket. It doesn't look good, doesn't look healthy.

As I turn on to Market Street I get an idea. I take out the fob but don't click its buttons. Instead I raise it to my mouth and say "testing" directly into it, as though it were recording me. Like the little Dictaphones my dad carried when I was a kid.

No one's startled. They walk straight by.

Back at the gallery, I talk politics with an artist, like me, quite visibly in the prime of his life. He works at the gallery and—since night has fallen—he offers me a drink. Like everyone over twenty-five, he and I talk about ourselves as though we're ancient.

"As I get older," he says, "I feel like I define myself by what I'm against." I tell him how it surprises me that my mind keeps changing instead of calcifying. Maybe being sick and having to adapt is a part of that. Lately, for example, I've quit bothering with Facebook, and for philosophical reasons. That surprises me about myself.

"Imagine being young with Facebook though," he says. "If it'd been around when we were young? These kids now are going to have to live with all their old pictures."

It's late and I'm relaxed, so I float a confession. "When someone friends me, I click the back arrow to see what their oldest picture is. To see who they used to be. Oh yeah, *that's* who you were."

The artist shakes his head. "You see who they were pretending to be."

On the train away from town, the 8:20 a.m. Downeaster, little jostles make me feel as though the world's about to pick up speed. Just as every time a movie begins to play, I release a little adrenalin—my body thinks the chair's moving and not the picture.

We're primed to expect one family of sickness story: descent and reemergence. This story may have two species, but both share traits. In one, the sufferer succumbs. If they were ready to go, that's a blessing; if they struggled, they fought bravely.

The other species of story is told by the sufferer. Here, the victim suffers, seeks healers, learns the way to health, and emerges with lessons, self knowledge, advice. This is the afternoon talk-show strain, the Louise Hay. In Hay's genre-founding bestseller, *You Too Can Change Your Life*, she describes the sixth sense, intuition, as both the cause and the cure of any variety of ill.

Vertigo is caused by "flighty, scattered thinking. A refusal to look." Deafness, she reveals, "is related to isolation and stubbornness and what you don't want to hear. Open yourself up to new ideas with the affirmation 'I listen to the Divine and rejoice at all that I am able to hear.'"

A woman named Beatrice runs a website on which she applies Hay's teaching to the various trials of Ménière's disease. Her story is that too many stressors were piling

up and causing her ears to run low on the right fuel. But
Beatrice—with Hay's help—took the matter in hand.
She wrote a newsletter to her family and friends "stating
my health issue and requesting that they keep their communication with me light & positive."

It won her, she tells us, three years symptom free. She
believed she could do it.

"Its navigational sense fucked up," Jeff says of the fork-
tailed flycatcher that's been gliding around the Audubon
sanctuary at the end of his street. The bird is South
American and, like a lot of South American birds, it's
flashier than its cold weather cousins. Midflight, the fil-
igreed tail feathers of the creature form a crescent of the
same size and arc as its wingspan: it looks like a bird flying alongside its own reflection. Or like two birds taking
off in different directions at the same time.

Jeff and I talk in the apartment above the gallery. He
moved to Portland from DC six months back and quit
his DC job as soon as he arrived. He's been spending the
days fishing for local work and chopping wood for the
winter. When he has enough wood for this year he starts
chopping wood for the next.

"It just flew thousands and thousands of miles in exactly the wrong direction," Jeff explains, "and it thinks
it's arrived in a place where it's just starting to be spring."

Audubon naturalists are conducting themselves as
gently as possible around tourists. "Where will it end

up?" one of them answered when prompted by a visitor: "Oh gosh, well maybe it'll learn to fly back home all of a sudden." When Jeff took a guide to one side, though, he was more forthright.

"When the snow comes, I would like whoever finds its body to let me know. I'd like to add it to our learning center."

"Did anyone say anything about me?" Peter asks. "I just wondered if Elizabeth had said something."

"Not a word." I knew he was the gallery's music programmer. And I could see with my own eyes he wore a mighty beard. I didn't know anything more.

He says, "I've been dealing with vertigo. Fortunately, it never happens for longer than twenty-four hours. I treat it like a migraine. But yeah."

"Oh shoot, that sucks. Was it the crystal misalignment thing?" Those otoliths.

"Yeah, the crystals. I mean, it feels weird to go to a doctor and have them tell you *Sir, you need to realign your crystals.*"

We talk about it a little more as I sip from my toucan mug. It's cold inside. I rub my hands together and wonder if Denver's turned me into a warm-weather wuss.

"I had to leave work last week," Peter says. "There wasn't any point in staying. I couldn't walk straight. When I tried to look at the computer it was just like ..." He holds his palms apart and tilts them, like he's showing off all the angles on a loaf of bread.

"So the room doesn't spin for you?"

"No, but it turns. My hearing is fine, so it's crystals. They give you a pamphlet with hilarious diagrams—positions you have to get in—but they work."

The ancient radiator clicks on behind me. I like that sound. We had radiators in my home as a kid, the clangs from nowhere and steam escapes turn the room into a kind of womb: the gastric burble and thrum of blood, the enveloping warmth.

"I shouldn't have driven a car," he says. "I mean, it's just like—blip: work, home. But I shouldn't have, probably. Everything tunneled. Walking to the car was like walking on a boat that keeps hitting waves. Driving was like that. Like when you want to go straight so you have to keep the wheel just so. A straight line wasn't straight."

There are days when the tongs and bones in my head fade to something unobtrusive—a background fridge. On some of those days my hearing loss falls from severe down to mild. Last time I had it tested on such a day I could make out 88 percent of the words the audiology tech spoke aloud, compared to 33 percent on a day that was worse. People with that level of hearing loss often get by without devices, and I take them off sometimes too. Maybe five afternoons a year.

I take them off at Bardo on such a day and the room sounds more real than a dream. Voices don't just carry information—they carry subtlety. A woman playing cards with her boyfriend laughs against him and I can hear the difference between indrawn air preceding a laugh and indrawn air proceeding speech. I can hear both his "guess I gotcha!" half-whistle inhale and the stomp of her foot as two different sounds, not one confusing sound.

Background music is glorious. All year I've only encountered it as an obstacle, something that would keep me from conversation, keep me from my thoughts. Now I remember why it's there. It doesn't get in the way; it just creates a mood. This stuff is some kind of C-grade reggae, but I love hearing it, love the faraway shout. It doesn't keep me from hearing an old student call my name across the room.

I walk better when I rise to say hello to her. How much more open spaces seem when I can hear the whole range of sounds in place! The echoes of sound—low ones, high ones—bouncing off all the surfaces orients us in space. We don't take that extra step back because we can hear someone approaching behind us. Sound is kinetic, and we use it to feel as much as hear.

Years earlier, when my symptoms intensified, I remember reading a comment on a Ménière's chat room where the author, from the depths of intractable vertigo, lamented her lot. "I've started hating the good days," she wrote, "because they remind me of what I've lost." I nodded yes as I read but only from indignation. I couldn't see how anyone could regret a good day.

My student turns out to have a head cold—I can hear the catch in her sinuses. The rustle of her newspaper folding up, the whisk of Kleenex from a plastic pouch,

the two-note *tock* of the ceramic cup she sets on the var-
nished wood of the table, all of them stand out on their
own. All of them convey information. None are distract-
ing or aggressive, none pull me away from my train of
thought. All of them welcome me into the world.

As I was growing up, my mother spoke of the deaths of
others with regret, but also circumspection. The name of
any illness was uttered in a whisper, and the name of the
most sinister—cancer—wasn't uttered at all. Likewise,
she thrilled each time a friend called to tell her they were
pregnant. It was no act: babies were the world's only un-
adulterated good.

Untimely death was bad—Mom believed that all
right—but the birth of a baby was more good than the
death was bad. The scales weren't entirely straight. This
unnerved me. One night we went to see a Tom Hanks
movie where he's teamed up with a dog. The dog and
Hanks were cop partners. Near the end, the dog is, of
course, shot and killed. I got up to wait in the lobby. I
didn't want to watch him buried with honors, thanks. I
had a dog of my own.

When they came out to fetch me my mother said,
"You shouldn't have been so worried about the dog dying.
It was okay at the end, because he had puppies."

It was *okay* at the end? Because other, totally different dogs had appeared? Dogs who *wouldn't even know
their father*? A few days later I remember saying, "Look,

one person's birth doesn't just make up for another person's death."

She regarded me with concern.

"Okay," I conceded, "but then if you think one makes up for the other, then neither is good and neither is bad, right? No cause for mourning or celebration? Then what's the point of anything?"

"That's a terrible thing to say."

The last day of the refugee class is a party, or the sort of thing teachers call a party. The students bring in food from their home cultures, laying it out on a long table in the back, then we all go around taking pictures. We watch the slideshows they put together as we sip Afghan chickpea soup and eat almond sweets from . . . Iraq?

"So many sweets!" Sara beams. "Lucky us, right?"

Socheat, from Cambodia, has been quiet for much of these eight weeks. She radiates thoughtfulness but keeps her own counsel, preferring not to speak rather than say the wrong thing. During her slideshow, the last of the presentations we watch, I find myself particularly caught up in her photo depiction of what life is like for her now, here in Denver.

The slide presents two pictures side by side, one color and one black and white. In the color picture, silver office towers loom over downtown, as though shot by someone on their back. Meanwhile, in the black-and-white picture beside it, a blindfolded woman navigates her way down a white hallway, her arms reaching toward, but not quite touching, the walls on either side.

The text beside it reads:

> I live with depression because I've become a person who doesn't understand the people around me, can't have a conversation. Sometimes, I feel like I've lost my hearing and sight because I can't understand when people are saying something and I can't understand what I read. I struggle when I work with people because I don't get all they're talking about.

When the lights come up and we all turn around to talk about their projects, I ask them how common that feeling is.

Yuliya from Ukraine raises her hand, "I have something to say on this subject." Haltingly—but less haltingly than she imagines—she explains that she used to study literature in Russia, and that here "it is difficult. Because I have all these thoughts. I want to say so *much*. But I don't have the word for what I want to say. And people think, 'Oh, well she must be stupid. She can't even talk.'"

I tell her I understand and that she'll get better as her new life goes on, that all of them will. But I know that at least one of them has been shown a gun by a neighbor and told to go back where she came from; as nothing is certain for anyone, so life is especially uncertain for them. The time to go arrives and they go.

. . .

Sound is not sound alone, it's touch. Waves of agitated air strike our bodies in patterns, and our bodies react to those patterns in the way we've trained them, or that we can't help.

Sufi theologian Ibn al-'Arabī defined the theological concept of *Barzakh* as a liminal space between the physical and the mystical world. We will arrive in Barzakh after death, but for Sufi mystics, Barzakh is also a place we can visit in our dreams or immersed in meditation.

Deborah Kapchan defines Barzakh as the place

> where material worlds are spiritualized and im-
> material worlds are made corporeal. It is a realm
> of vibration, sometimes taking color and shape,
> sometimes sounded, sometimes ineffable but felt.

Music is how a Sufi crosses to Barzakh—music and dance.

I wasn't ever nuts about punk rock shows. They were fun if you abandoned yourself to thrashing, but I couldn't keep that up for long. My thoughts dream off into the distance and then return to me in different shapes; I like music for exactly that reason—the way it carries thoughts off and returns them—but punk music seemed to keep them from coming back, wall them up in the noise. That used to panic me.

There's a punk show underneath me tonight at the gallery downstairs. I'm not wearing hearing aids so the music is faint; the bass, on the other hand, feels reverberant. Fish have sound receptors along the length of their bodies. Humans only feel bass notes in their whole bodies when those bass notes are awfully loud.

When the strings of the bass are plucked, those strings vibrate. The pattern of those vibrations feeds down a wire that hums before a sympathetic magnet, creating a magnetic field. That signal travels along new wires to the amplifier, which in turn vibrates the diaphragms of the four QSC subwoofers strategically positioned around the gallery downstairs. Tonight, Peter tells me, is the first night all four of them will be online.

As the band, a local outfit called Mouth Washington, generates low tones with bass drum and strings, the subwoofers vibrate at those frequencies, launching cyclic ripples through the air around the stage, the bodies of listeners, and the wooden floor beneath my chair. The floor beneath me becomes a diaphragm, reverberating with loud, complex waves. The air in the room moves invisibly, distance between the peaks in the waves flattening out as they swim toward the roof.

Standing on the floor above a concert feels like sitting in a car—the vibrations make me feel as though I'm traveling.

I'm fascinated by all this movement in a room that was quiet ten minutes before. The violet-tipped beak of the toucan on my coffee mug vibrates along with the unfinished desk it's resting atop and the plywood floorboards beneath it. The old metal chair where I'm sitting vibrates too, and my body vibrates—I conduct the sound.

Bass guitars are capable of playing as low as 36 Hz—a sound at the far low end of what humans can hear. When those waves mix and fray they can reach lower still. Thanks to the subwoofers' 130 dB power, they can perfectly replicate the sound of thunder, and its own vibrations.

Movement blurs the room. A sense of urgency holds me still. It can't get out of my head.

And then my body surprises me, responding with vertigo. The lighted kitchen counter I can see from where I sit, and the lima bean–colored wall behind it, trail off to the right together and keep moving. They travel right, right: somehow returning to move again, as though a photograph copied itself at a rate twice that of resting pulse, each new copy fanning rightward and vanishing. Into what?

On another night this would panic me. I'd be panicked if I was working on deadline or if I had evening plans or if I had to do anything the following day that required concentration. But I'm not panicked now. The vertigo is not bad, for one: I can walk as though on a tossing ship—the waves aren't strong enough to toss me overboard.

Was this a wave effect of the notes downstairs, a certain frequency reverberating through fluid in my ears in the same way buildings can be taken apart by sinister frequencies of wind? Every glass can be destabilized by the right frequency—can every Ménière's-addled ear?

Or was this merely a trick of the eye that went too far? In the same way a moving car, viewed from a car at rest, can trigger mild vertigo from time to time, did the movement around me startle my ailing vestibular system into panic? I don't know. I can't know. I haven't met a doctor who'd be curious enough to devise a test.

So the question plays out in my mind, where it can play for as long as it likes. I'm content tonight to watch the room hum away from me, the motion of waves coursing through every cell of my body at three hundred meters per second. I don't panic.

And then my next life begins.

Shocked Quartz

As we cross into New Mexico the land flattens into pla-
teau. Juniper and cottonwood from El Greco, waist-high
scrub. It's a landscape famous from gelatin silver prints
edged with rearing mesas—they take forever to grow
close. They fall away.

It's always felt lonely to me, too empty. I know this is
a bigotry; I know that what seems lifeless is filled with
life: collared lizards and whip snakes, making shelter under the scrub and drinking morning dew from its leaves.
I wish I could feel what other visitors say they feel, what
Elisa on our first date called the "mystique of the desert,"
the kind of transcendence I know from long walks in the
northern woods, but colored differently, default beiges,
surfaces dry enough you can feel the dryness without
touching them.

My ears—good when we started—begin to fuzz out
south of Pueblo. Long trips do this: vibrations, elevation changes, something. Because music's unsettling we

eschew it for reading aloud. She's driving and I've got *Black Water*, a long book of ghost stories. Stuff with names like "The Door in the Wall," and "The Signalman." Elisa laughs at the scary parts, "This is so stupid!" She's having fun. We both are. We're on our way to the Albuquerque International Balloon Fiesta, an annual launch, the biggest in the world, where six hundred hotair balloons lift off at once from a park just north of the city. A whole group of us pooled for a rental for two nights. I fully expect something transcendent: desert transcendence—mysteries above to match the mysteries below.

Under the macadam beneath the tires and beneath the hard rock under that, sleeps—and has long slept—the secret history of life on earth. If we were to turn the car to the right, by evening we'd reach the Barringer Crater, site of the first discovery of shocked quartz, the place where the theory of planetary catastrophism was more or less proved.

Why can we find seashells in the desert? What killed the terrible lizards that walked the earth? In the 1830s Georges Cuvier, father of paleontology, thought he'd found the answer. He described what he called a series of "revolutions of the earth," sweeping changes caused by asteroids, volcanos, climate catastrophe.

But the zeitgeist wasn't ready for planetary catastrophes. We're accustomed to the idea now, but for a world that had struggled to stop believing in miracles, the idea of catastrophic extinction must have been terrifying. Charles Lyell, Charles Darwin's teacher, maintained his own principal, which comes down to us as "uniformitarianism"—the idea that the past closely resembled the present; changes in the earth weren't quick or random but gradual, the working out of nature's plan. Lyell thought dinosaurs would return again, after an epochs-long slumber. Saner heads thought Lyell a little mad but understood "revolutions in the earth" to be nonsense: earth cycles were rational, you see; they worked according to a preordained plan; it made all the sense in the world that lumbering lizards would step aside to make way for us because we were more perfect. Like empires, species entered their dotage and declined. Or else, yes, God had a slow plan. History had a set course, an arrow. Anything but comets from the sky. Anything but luck.

Arroyos. A little shortgrass. Casinos appear and an overpass darkens our car. Inside the casa we find our friends and their friends distributed on chairs and sofas, watching a tattoo show: skulls, eyeballs, fantasy girls. The sound of it comes at me like a wall but that wall isn't real—if I unclipped these hearing aids what seemed like heavy air would retreat back into the set, become quaint, a little chatter in a box.

"Want us to turn this down? Turn it up?"

"Subtitles, John? Let's get subtitles for John."

I listen to the conversation merge with the wall of words and music from the show, *Competition butter-flies itssourer weatherpillow. I'm definitely freakinthe-roseoutofyourhair.*

"Dome competition?"

"Strange brooch."

It's fine. Life's dull without mystery.

"Did one of you say dome?"

"Dumb. Look at that thing he's making!"

I ask Mike where I should throw our stuff and he gets up to show me. Mike is a PhD student, a polymath. I can still keep up with such a person, mostly because neither of us is too concerned if we don't understand what the other says.

"Due to your late arrival, you and Elisa did wind up with the smallest room," Mike says. "But it's got a bed. And a door! You have a door."

I pretend Mike is a porter, handing him my bags. He pretends he is a porter and carries them into the small room. Stucco, skylight askew, the lines of its frame rounded to resemble adobe, like you could carve sharp corners but you hadn't yet.

"There is a courtyard," Mike said. It pleases him to show me around, so he takes me out back. The courtyard is pebbly, severe in the afternoon light, almost medieval—like lots of southwestern design—in its asceticism. I worry the kind of pleasure you'd find here is Saint Augustine's variety—where knotted rope is a sign of the devil's work and only straight rope wards him off.

I say, "It's like a monk's cell."

Mike pats my back. "The only way to go is up."

As we move from the courtyard to the living room to the bar outside the Hotel St. Francis we grow more excited about tomorrow's trip. The balloons launch early—something to do with the early wind. Each of us takes turns trying to explain it. We're staying in Santa Fe, so we'll be driving an hour south. That's a 4:30 a.m. wakeup.

"They're not all balloon shaped. They've got houses, cats, like tigers—"

"I saw them on PBS when I was little."

Everyone's fine with sitting outside where I can hear. I'm so happy to understand their voices I sit still as I can to listen.

"Is the idea you lie on your back when they take off, watch them all just appear?"

I make a joke: "You could do that, the rattlesnakes are probably still slow at 6 a.m."

I sip a Muscadet. Yes, my ears are bad, cottony, and clicking from the trip, but such unsettling numbers of disabled people live in isolation, or can't find work, or can't get to work. Their rights are being rolled back. I know fate's favored me relative to other sufferers: I can sit on this balcony, go to sleep next to Elisa, wake up, be a part of something bigger than myself, even if it's only a tourist fair.

Mike's looking at his phone. He starts to speak, drawing out the first vowel. "I—don't wanna be a buzzkill but if we're getting up at four thirty . . ."

The square's not crowded. The ground has given up the day's heat. On the walk to the house I trip over a sidewalk protrusion and realize, a moment after Elisa does, that there was no protrusion there. I saw a mirage. The ground isn't steady.

"Are you okay?"

"Maybe yes, maybe no."

She takes my arm as we fall behind the others.

"You only had one drink?"

"It's not the drink." It's travel or it isn't. It's the spicy dinner we ate or it's something else. Back at the house, I lie down in the dark bedroom and the skylight unsettles itself to the right, to the right. I lie there without control of my eyes. Elisa gets ready for bed in the dark, lies down beside me.

I say, "This isn't over yet. I can't wake up at four. I can't . . . I'm going to be a wreck at the balloon fair. Oh, Christ, we came all this way for this."

Vertigo is less frequent, but it still happens. Will it continue to come and go as it did for Jonathan Swift three hundred years ago, until I'm senseless and alone? Or, once my ears hear no more, will the dizziness stop for good then too? Did I do anything to call this upon myself? Will total deafness come on me suddenly— waking up one morning with no sound in either ear—or will it steal over me by stages? Will the vertigo again become acute? Will the stress of this, or some root cause that spurs it, end my life before it might otherwise end? When will I hear my last strain of music? If harm befalls Elisa, will I be healthy enough to take care of her?

Carolyn warns me against what she calls *catastrophizing*: "Sometimes your health may make something impossible," she tells me. "This is unpredictable and it's alarming, but that doesn't mean that *everything* is impossible. It doesn't mean you won't have good days. It doesn't mean you need to panic."

She interrupts herself. "Do you know about the sympathetic nervous system? Do this—next time your heart is racing, do this." She makes a temple of her fingers above her chest, both hands, lets them rise and fall against her chest like she's miming the beat of her own heart. "Lub-dub. Lub-dub. Just like that, lub-dub. One beat per second. That's resting heart rate. If both your arms are as high as your chest—both elbows up, like this—your heart will slow down."

"Why?"

"Because it's all connected. It's sympathetic."

"I mean why me?"

She speaks slower, the way I speak to someone who's upset. But we're not upset.

"You *know* why this happened to you. It's just bad luck."

Accidents, coincidence. We're careful with mirrors. We blow on the dice.

This is one of the reasons it's surprising that even Darwin had trouble with Cuvier's catastrophe theory. Darwin understood the role of luck at the species level: one kind of weasel didn't become another kind of weasel because it was especially industrious or faithful but because the environment changed and new skills were required to survive. Or because a few weasels wandered off from the pack and were forced into isolation. Or because the female of the species developed a kink.

I wonder if Darwin's failure to embrace the catastrophe theory didn't lend more respectability to the social-Darwinist argument from later years, "race science," the ugly and perfectly American idea that the wealthiest own the largest part of virtue. Health becomes a virtue. Good looks become a virtue. If you flaunt it you deserved to get it. Only haters hate. Justice is for the jealous.

Catastrophism puts paid to all this prosperity gospel: species, it turns out, survive catastrophes for no fore-ordained reason. Likewise, I didn't have to survive the crisis of my own life so far. I could have managed it better or worse, but the ways in which I did so would have been out of my hands. I believe this, even if I need to be reminded.

I sleep when the window high up quits moving. What seems a few seconds later, Elisa wakes me up without meaning to. She's getting dressed, unzipping and zipping her suitcase quietly as she gropes for her clothes in the dark. The floorboards creek as she pads around the bed.

My hearing's sharp in the wake of vertigo attacks. No one's sure why. It's always been like that. And so I hear Elisa's voice at 5 a.m. without machines. I hear it the way I used to.

"It's okay, sweetie. Just stay here and rest. We'll be back in a few hours."

I could come if I wanted, feel sick and exhausted at the fair, but part of living a good life is not heaving that strain onto others, not acting like I'm immortal. Letting them go.

Life has every mystery. This event I miss, the balloons in the air, the ecstatic moment, is merely one of millions of things I can't access—the mind of a bat, the pattern of this small gust about to touch me. No one can visit all the cities—we take them on faith. We'll never count the species that once survived on earth.

I sleep without dreaming for hours.

I open my eyes. The room is white from the light cast by that one piece of glass in the ceiling. The clock says it's nearly 12:00 p.m.

Amazingly, my ears are still good—not as good as when Elisa left the house, but the roar is so low it's only nominally there. I can make out traffic sounds, the hum of pipes in the wall. I take up my headphones and my phone and make for that courtyard.

Late morning, late September. The air is hot in the dry way of an empty stove. Pebbles underfoot, iron sculptures half-made and half-found, a bit of bicycle. As I step outside something exits—a gecko?—I won't know. I stare for a minute, waiting for it to return. Life is all around me, hiding. The ground beneath me is a library of which anyone can only read a part, a few shelves.

At the end of the K-T catastrophe, the asteroid that wiped out most of the life on earth, a few animals managed to survive thanks to the pure luck of their habitat, their location on the globe, their source of food. Ten thousand years later—no time at all—and the earth had recovered, albeit changed. The earth was alive as it had ever been, but with new creatures, however subtly new. Indistinguishably new at first, they grew stranger with time.

I set headphones in place and resync them with the Bluetooth on my phone to play the track I've been saving for a moment like this: Anna Maria Friman, a Swedish soprano. The song is an Italian *lauda*, a Renaissance street song. This one, "Ave Vergene gaudente," is devotional, probably to Mary (probably asking her to put in a word with Christ). I don't speak Italian but I'm not interested in what the words mean so much as I am the sound of them, as Gavin Bryars set them and as Friman sends them up through the clear glass well of her voice.

There's no shade. I don't need shade—I'm pale as this page. I sit back in a wooden chair and send the volume up. I soak in the heat.

Ave. Vergene. The words, all vowel, liquid syllables falling over one another appear. The bells of my ears set them ringing through my body.

The silence behind her voice is beautiful: an echo at the ready, a vault or the sound of a vault. Like someone set a candle on the floor and the smoke rose and curled. You don't see the wind without it—the wind's too light to see.

Mike and Elisa and the rest will be back in an hour. They'll tell me about the chaos of finding each other ("We're under the frog but the frog's going due south!"). We'll play two-handed poker, find a hidden door to the cellar. We'll laugh at one another.

Alone for the moment, I tap the volume as high as it goes. I want to be enveloped. My eyes squint in pleasurable pain. Her voice gets sharp by going high. Every line opens with a thin loud vowel.

Desert heat, ancient music, I suffer a rush of awe.

Full sun at noon.

Coda

When I moved to Colorado I was working on a novel, my second novel, now abandoned: a man arrives in Denver, alone, pursued by ghosts. These ghosts take the form of past adversaries, sad parents, foiled romances, canceled friendships. They dog him, calling late, waiting outside the classes he teaches to bark at him, materializing in the middle of the street to startle his car off the road. The book was intended as funny. The ghosts were opera buffa, burlesques of ghosts. It wasn't working, but I assumed I'd have plenty of time to alter the story, take a year or two to run through drafts. The Colorado sky, gessoed with snow, was a blank notebook page. There were plenty of pages. The notebook was new.

Within a few months the story escaped me. Life was eaten by bottles of pills and medical electronics and five new bills in the mail per day—many of them duplicates of older bills, but you had to be sure. They covered the dining room table. Elisa and I had talked about the idea of having children, but this was not the time. It never became time. Those ghosts from my novel kept me company as I sat up spinning in the night. They told me I'd lived the wrong life till then, and it was too late now, *too late*. At night, my hearing aids snapped tight into their chipped-up leather case on the sill, I listened to the skirl in my head. It wouldn't have felt so unnerving if I could make out sounds aside from the feedback my brain kicked up, confused; in the dark it made a cosmos. All of our bodies hide these secrets: the cancer that's going to rear up, the curve that's tensing in your spine. The body I'd relied on attacked me—my self had attacked my self—such that I didn't know what I could trust.

On days when I could leave the house I carried a knife in my pocket so I could maintain the option of jabbing it into my own throat. I'd reach into the pocket of my coat, fold and unfold the blade from its handle—stainless steel, serrated—as a tic. How long would it take to bleed out? The TV star who'd cut his own throat fifteen minutes from my childhood house had died right away. Would I die right away? I'd walk far from our building so Elisa wouldn't find me. At another bad-news doctor's appointment, shortly after what felt like a catastrophic failure at the Mayo Clinic and an avalanche of loneliness on the plane home, it took all the will I could muster not to reach into my pocket and hold the knife up to my neck, threaten to drive it in if the doctor didn't find something to make the ratcheting sound in my head go away, please. I wanted to say *my life is in your hands*. If this sounds melodramatic, that wasn't lost on me. I gave Elisa the knife and told her to hide it or throw it away. When I visited my parents—gun owners—I made them lock the pump-action and the Walther PPK in the trunk of the car. My mother drove them to a neighbor's house, said she didn't want them back.

Had I acted, I'd have hurt the people who survived me, who loved me. I told myself—and this felt true—that they didn't love the man I was becoming, only loved the person I used to be. New John, sick John—the one who couldn't hear them, who needed to be cared for, could better their lives only by vanishing. It took time to discern that killing myself would hurt them worse than living: it wouldn't just burden them, it would accuse them. After months of grim talks with old friends and bewildered family, I knew I had to at least try to get my mind someplace else, even if it was mere distraction. Even if it was meds. I called my insurance company for a list of psychologists. In a mansion on Denver's Capitol Hill, a tall woman with sympathetic eyes asked me a few simple questions over the course of half an hour then leaned forward and said, "It sounds like you're lonely and you're scared. You're probably angry. I'm happy to talk about all this."

I liked her immensely. But she wasn't taking Blue Cross insurance anymore. I kept looking. I tried a psychiatrist next, in a high rise on the other side of Speer Boulevard.

"Did you get along with your dad?" he asked. "I mean, as a kid?"

I said we could talk about childhood plenty later. First I had to explain what was going on with my ears.

"I ask," he said, "because my own dad used to hit me with a closed fist." He punched his palm.

Several names later, I found Carolyn.

"You've got a chronic illness," Carolyn said, "and now you've got to think of yourself at age ninety. You could very well reach ninety, if you don't kill yourself first, and so you've got to keep in mind the wellbeing of that ninety-year-old man. Try to think kindly of that little man. Right now, I get the sense that you're angry with him for having a chronic illness. Because he's disappointing you. You have to be more compassionate with him." Her language was measured, weighted to soothe. What she was telling me about myself tomorrow, myself next year and years after, was that I ought not to fear him, the way I feared—in 2013, when I first became sick—the person who writes these words.

Instead of talking about my illness as much as I'd talked about it in 2013 (to the distress of my listener), I grew more private with my complaints and fears and regrets; what I would once have spoken now I wrote. Those notes became a book. I tried to trace the story as a way of seeing where it pointed. In the bad summer, the summer all trace of hearing in both ears vanished for a week, I dragged myself into the study to write at least one paragraph a day. When I wrote about going deaf at the University of Colorado, I told the truth but omitted the story of how I drove home in a late snowstorm two weeks earlier, how the roar in my ears occluded the audiobooks I'd been using to replace music. As often happens in stop-start traffic, what looked like the easing of

congestion suddenly tightened again, the car coming out
of my control when the breaks locked and nearly sliding
beneath the trailer ahead. It wasn't vertigo, it was ice; my
body really *was* moving. But the loss of control reminded
me of vertigo. Once the actual vertigo started up a week
later, I felt superstitiously afraid I'd called it on myself.

In the months that followed, the nightmare of spinning, I caught my brain rolling back—loose as my eyes in
their sockets—to moments I wished I might have lived
over. My childhood: the boys and girls I should have
befriended, or kissed, or finally fought off, the dumb
remarks, the nights everyone went out and I stayed in
and regretted it. The pages I should have filled. The raw
wasted time. I consoled myself that at least I'd learn all
that could be learned about the disease—or collection
of diseases catalogued uneasily under the name of one
nineteenth century Parisian. Unrelatedly—or relatedly,
there is no one who can say—the vertigo attacks largely
abated in the course of my writing. They will surely return. I'll write while I can.

No longer able to teach large classes, I taught small
workshop classes, took on freelance editing work, a little
ghostwriting. It wasn't enough—it's still not enough—
but since I could work nearly anywhere I worked at
Bardo, on the beat-up sofa in the back. One afternoon
the stranger across me started crying. She'd just arrived
in Denver from Australia and she felt as though she'd
screwed up her life. She felt hopeless. I told her my own
story, told her I was trying to find ways to go on. By the
time she left she was thanking me, "just for listening."

A voice to my left: "So are you just, like, really into Jonathan Swift?"

It was the philosophy student at the next sofa. She was wearing slippers, reading Deleuze and Guattari. I didn't know her that evening, but in a matter of months she became one of my closest friends. By way of introduction I told her why I was reading about Swift—about the vertigo—and she told me about hanging upside down and spinning on aerial silks at a circus in Johannesburg. The next night an older trans woman sat across from us and the three of us talked philosophy—mostly throwing the names of post-structuralists at one another—until nearly 2 a.m. Life is fascinating. I'd been so down on myself about my illness—what it had taken from me—I felt half amazed three strangers would want to talk to me so long and so late. I'd forgotten I had any worth, that I wasn't just a set of bad sensations in the dark.

The next day I drove to the airport to collect Elisa. She'd been out of town all week. I *drove* to the airport. I was reentering the world—partially because my ears weren't giving me such a bad time and partially because I'd found ways to adjust. We got a booth at a restaurant on the way home and I sat on her side of it not only to hear her better but to touch her hair and put my arm around her. It's not given to every marriage to be happy, but I found myself—I find myself—wrapped up in a rush of love toward Elisa. I have this pause in deterioration, this time to adjust—but to what? I have to make the most of it. I'll practice compassion, I'll keep from expressing resentment toward the healthy-eared and well-balanced, or from turning my bitterness inward, back to the knife. Elisa never had to prove herself to me, but she proved herself to me these last years. I want to prove myself to her.

Following my visit to Fort Lyon, learning firsthand the way bad luck can alter the chemistry of the brain, I came to understand how this condition, the force of it, had denatured me. I accepted that the lost time was now lost, that the possibilities remaining in my life were narrower. (All of this took time; all of this was attrition.) What I took to be triage—hearing aids, a pocketful of Valium, time each day to rest—was in fact the scaffolding of my new life. And if the body is the self, if the body is the mind, then the hearing aids behind my ears and the lassitude that fell on me and the sounds in my head were my new bones and skin. I had to choose the way I'd be in the world with them.

Compassion for the world, over which we have only narrow dominion, and awe at the world's mutability, can germinate in the cultivation of a gentleness in one's self, a gentleness for one's future self, over which we have only narrow dominion. In feeling a little sorry for myself, I also feel sorry for the world, the evening world of half measures and regrets, the morning world when we sweep up and start again. If my ears go bad—the now-familiar procession of ordinance and whistles—or if the world tips over and I feel like I'm falling, I don't blame myself, my body. I've lost so much time to the illness I'm jealous of the time that remains. When it's over, I tell myself, I can call up a sinister friend for some oxycodone. I never make the call.

. . .

Not long after I first fell ill, I met an old Denver lawyer named Tim for a drink. I was still figuring out what I could take into my body and what I couldn't. I ordered a soda water. All my conversation in those days was about the thing happening to my ears.

"So what's your plan?" Tim asked.

I didn't have an answer. I knew what the plan wasn't. I wasn't going to stoically play some kind of hero—I'm a good actor but not a great one. I also wasn't going to endanger people around me by trying to live as though I wasn't ill: frequent driving, applying for jobs that required I fake my way through phone calls, throwing up from dizziness in stranger's homes. This would be jock courage, the man struck blind who attempts to repair his wounded ego by endangering the lives of a half dozen Sherpa guides and rescue teams and climbing Everest. Life-as-inspirational-poster. I felt like I'd been bad company for Tim that afternoon, but he didn't give up on me. Not long ago he took a writing class I taught—a class where I recited the same lines of *Hamlet* two different ways to show off the difference between a mimetic and a presentational style of telling. Tim watched me teach like a cowboy might watch a group of newcomers pour off a train. After class we ate lunch outdoors and away from the street so I could hear him. We talked about writing. I talked about how writing a book had made me more passionate about life, all parts of it but especially putting words together. How even though music had largely vanished, the shuffle of words into lines revealed itself as the music I wouldn't lose.

Tim has a marvelous self-possession, speaks in a way that no one from the cities of my youth ever spoke: he thinks first, choosing words with the care of a pool sharp choosing a cue, and you can see him thinking. This poses a danger because, should I fail to hear what he says on first pass, he may want to rethink it, may take his time.

"When I met you, where was that place we met? Oh yeah. You were in a bad place," he said. "You . . . were scared. It's a pleasure to see . . . you just seem *alive* now."

I told him thanks. I told him people like himself—or like the couple who run Lighthouse and keep inviting me back to teach, or like my coffee shop friend, Tiffany, who built me a new desk to drain the bad energy from the room where I'd lain so long sick—had lent me courage, because all of them befriended me, continued to solicit my company, even though they had met me after the illness. They never knew me before, never knew the boy in black boots who smoked cigarettes and drank whiskey, who liked loud parties, whose most significant talent was an ability to hear the subtleties in the voices of others such that he could impersonate them later, the corners of voices no one else noticed, the secrets of speech.

That youth, with his preoccupations and disquiets, is gone.

What's the story of my life? Discrete, not continuous.

Thus play I in one person many people.

I'm writing now from a broken car seat outside St. Mark's Coffee House. It's the last warm day of autumn— eighty degrees today, but the barometer is already dropping, the wind's picking up, snow's coming.

My friend Michael stopped by a few minutes ago. Michael has a Hollywood smoothness about him. He used to star in a daytime soap on CBS, *Capitol*, until it was replaced by *The Bold and the Beautiful*. The cancelation wasn't why he gave up acting. He quit to look after his son, diagnosed at a young age with cancer.

"I felt—and I wasn't the one who was sick, it was so much worse for my son—but I felt awful for him, and I just felt like I was in a *trench*. The sky was above me but it was far up there. I turned my head left and right and all I could see on both sides were the dirt walls of the trench. But, as he survived and recovered, gradually I came to realize the ground was sloping up."

"That's a good metaphor."

All around us, partly stubbed cigarettes smolder in ashtrays; their owners retreated inside with the change of air.

"I see you there now," Michael says. "You may not be out of the trench yet but—"

"But I'm only buried up to my chest."

I start packing up my things to walk home. First I take both hearing aids from my ears and snap them into their case. This makes the roar in my ears louder too, but at the same time it dampens the construction sounds from across the street, the fighter-plane boom the machines make of traffic, the wind like crumpling paper.

I walk home past the brew pub, the ice cream shop, the homeless man with the malformed leg. I give him a dollar, remember to shake his hand. I pass the mortuary on Seventeenth and Josephine, startled again by the weightless thing I made of death only a few years back. I had to suffer so badly it altered my chemistry—fragile at the best of times—pumped me full of cortisone and turned my furious emotion black and white. I hope that's over. It's over for the time being.

Turning onto Colfax, I want to cry thinking of how I almost lost Elisa, and the world, so deliberately; how I almost forced her to lose me. (I take pills to keep me from crying; I walk home composed.) My grip—the grip of this *self* with the noise in his head—is only so strong. We lease our own bodies. I want to stay in mine longer now. I don't want to lose it.

In the end I'll step through my own front door, returned through veils of dumb luck to the woman who loves me, to the study we've refurnished. After dinner, Elisa will read on the couch across from my desk, where I'll sit and make notes for another book. I've never liked writing about writing—it feels like staring at the sun, tempting fate. But I am drafting stories—not the old stories: new stories, sharper stories. There's so much I can't do that the things I can do—this one thing—rises up at me with more urgency. It moves my arms and legs. It agitates the air.

I feel older but I'm alive. I want to make something new, something other than the book in your hands. Far from wanting to stop time, I want more time. It passes, even through pain.

Notes

All of the stories in this book have been reported to the best of my recollection, sometimes while they were happening, sometimes after a span of years. I have distributed pseudonyms to some characters—for my college students and the residents of Fort Lyon, I have done this in every case—and I have smudged some identities where it seemed prudent to do so.

With the exception of short quotations from famous poems by Swift or Yeats or Shakespeare, those passages of the book that rely on external sources are all marked and noted below. However, in the case of two books—Leo Damrosch's *Jonathan Swift: His Life and His World*, and Robert W. Baloh's *Vertigo: Five Physician Scientists and the Quest for a Cure*—this style of citation is insufficient to communicate my debt. Both books were by my side throughout the writing of "The Hundred Oceans of Jonathan Swift." I could not have done it without them.

3   *"Illness and Paris"* From Xavier Aubryet, "La Maladie à Paris," cited in Alphonse Daudet, *In the Land of Pain*, trans. Julian Barnes (New York: Alfred A. Knopf, 2002).

21   *"It is hearing that contributes"* Aristotle, "On Sense and the Sensible," in *Short Treatises on Nature*, trans. J. I. Beare,

accessed on the Internet Classics Archive, http://classics.
mit.edu/Aristotle/sense.mb.txt.

24   *There's little in ancient Greek* Croesus, king of Lydia, had
        two sons, Atys ("as fine a young man as one could fancy")
        and a deaf son who, tellingly, goes unnamed. Croesus
        tells Atys, "You are my only son, for I do not count that
        wretched cripple, your brother." To give Herodotus his
        due as an ironist, that deaf son goes on to save his father's
        life (and from then on is granted the power of speech,
        although Herodotus is silent about whether the boy's abil-
        ity to hear is also changed). It's a story about fate, about
        calling no man happy until he dies. Until he's cold in the
        ground, you can only say of a man that he is "lucky." All
        of this from Aubrey de Sélincourt's translation, revised
        by A. R. Burn, of *Herodotus: The Histories* (New York:
        Penguin Books, 1972).

27   *"which partakes"* Nancy Mairs, "On Being a Cripple," in
        The Norton Reader: An Anthology of Nonfiction, ed. Linda
        Peterson et al., 13th ed. (New York: W. W. Norton, 2001).

37   *"It's not unusual"* Katherine Bouton, *Shouting Won't Help:
        Why I—and 50 Million Other Americans—Can't Hear You*
        (New York: Sarah Crichton Books, 2013).

48   *"one of the oldest"* Peter N. Stearns, *Shame: A Brief History*
        (Urbana: University of Illinois Press, 2017).

50   *"Music is heard perfectly"* Kenneth W. Berger, *The Hearing
        Aid: Its Operation and Development* (Detroit, MI: The
        National Hearing Aid Society, 1970).

50   *From the 1860s to the 1970s* Susan M. Schweik, *The
        Ugly Laws: Disability in Public* (New York: New York
        University Press, 2009).

55   *Early dementia is troublingly common* Frank R. Lin et
        al., "Hearing Loss and Incident Dementia," *Archives
        of Neurology* 68, no. 2 (2011): 214–20, doi:10.1001/
        archneurol.2010.362.

56   *the reason so many accidents happen* Brett E. Kemker et
        al., "Effects of a Cell Phone Conversation on Cognitive
        Processing Performances," *Journal of the American Academy of
        Audiology* 20, no. 9 (2009): 582–88, doi:10.3766/jaaa.20.9.6.

59　*"In my eyes he matches the gods"* Sappho, *The Poetry of Sappho*, trans. Jim Powell (New York: Oxford University Press, 2007).

63　**On March 24, 2004** Rod Antone and Leila Fujimori, "Suicide Note Turns Up in Fire," *Honolulu Star-Bulletin*, March 24, 2004, http://archives.starbulletin.com/2004/03/24/news/story1.html. Also: Rod Antone, "Deaths Deemed Murder-Suicide," *Honolulu Star-Bulletin*, March 25, 2004, http://archives.starbulletin.com/2004/03/25/news/story4.html.

65　*"Meanwhile," Elisa read* Wallace Shawn, *The Designated Mourner: A Play* (New York: Farrar, Straus and Giroux, 1996). All quotations from the play follow this edition.

78　*"If you stood"* Natsume Sōseki, *The Three Cornered World*, trans. Alan Turney (Washington, DC: Gateway Editions, 1965).

82　*"Jesus Christ, will you stop bothering me?"* Shawn, *Designated Mourner*.

89　*"court of last resort"* Leonard Berry and Kent Seltman, *Management Lessons from Mayo Clinic: Inside One of the Most Admired Service Organizations* (New York: McGraw Hill Education, 2017).

97　**See James Gillray's 1802 illustration** Available at the Morgan Library Museum online: https://www.themorgan.org/blog/cow-pock-or-wonderful-effects-new-inoculation.

100　*"raise their eyes"* Berry and Seltman, *Management Lessons from Mayo Clinic*.

107　**We don't really know** Barbara Woodward Lips Patient Education Center, "Patient Education: Chronic Subjective Dizziness" (Rochester, MN: Mayo Foundation for Medical Education and Research, 2011).

109　*"a standard treatment"* Berry and Seltman, *Management Lessons from Mayo Clinic*.

135　*"Coolness—"* Yosa Buson, in *The Essential Haiku: Versions of Bashō, Buson, and Issa*, trans. Robert Hass (New York: Ecco, 1994).

149　*"Jack of die"* Alice Notley, "In the Pines," in *In the Pines* (New York: Penguin Books, 2007).

158   *There's a brief questionnaire* For more informa-
       tion about the ACE test, visit https://www.cdc.gov/
       violenceprevention/aces/.

166   *"You take all the people"* Evan S. Connell, "The Beau
       Monde of Mrs. Bridge," in *The Collected Stories of Evan S.
       Connell* (Berkeley, CA: Counterpoint, 1995).

167   *"Other studies have found"* Robert H. Frank, *Success and
       Luck: Good Fortune and the Myth of Meritocracy* (Princeton,
       NJ: Princeton University Press, 2016).

183   *"I should then see"* For all quotations from *Gulliver's
       Travels* I use the 2003 Penguin Classics edition, edited by
       Robert Demaria, Jr., based on the first edition of *Travels
       into Several Remote Nations of the World in Four Parts by
       Lemuel Gulliver, First a Surgeon, and Then a Captain of
       Several Ships* (London: Benjamin Motte, 1726).

183   *"Oh! Faith"* W. R. Wilde, *The Closing Years of Dean Swift's
       Life; with an Appendix Containing Several of His Poems
       Hitherto Unpublished and Some Remarks on Stella* (Dublin,
       Ireland: Hodges and Smith, 1848).

194   *"Meaning structures"* Havi Carel, "Living in the Present:
       Illness, Phenomenology, and Well-Being," in *The
       Routledge History of Disease*, ed. Mark Jackson (London:
       Routledge, 2017).

198   *"my ears continue"* David Wyn Jones, *The Life of Beethoven*
       (Cambridge, UK: Cambridge University Press, 1998). I
       don't remember which edition of the letters I pulled from
       the shelf at Harvard, but Jones's book is where I later con-
       firmed the phrasing.

202   *"hundred golden pippins"* Jonathan Swift to Henrietta
       Howard, August 19, 1727, in *Correspondence of Jonathan
       Swift, D.D.*, ed. David Woolley, vol. III (Frankfurt am
       Main, Germany: Peter Lang, 2003).

203   *Temple's illegitimate daughter* Leo Damrosch, *Jonathan
       Swift: His Life and His World* (New Haven, CT: Yale
       University Press, 2013).

204   *"this morning, sitting in my bed"* Jonathan Swift, *Journal to
       Stella* (Chicago: Academy Chicago Publishers, 1986).

205 *"Overloading the stomach"* Wilde, *Closing Years.*

206 *"The origin of diseases"* Samuel Johnson, *Lives of the English Poets,* completed by William Hazlitt, vol. 3 (London: Nathaniel Cooke, 1854).

206 *a Philadelphia ophthalmologist* George M. Gould, *The Case of Jonathan Swift* (St. Louis, MO: Interstate Medical Journal Co., 1908).

207 *"If you and she"* William Butler Yeats, "The Words on the Window-Pane," in *The Collected Plays of W.B. Yeats* (New York: Macmillan, 1934).

207 *"I used to be free"* Jonathan Swift to Knightley Chetwode, January 30, 1721-2, in *Correspondence of Jonathan Swift, D.D.,* ed. David Woolley, vol. II (Frankfurt am Main, Germany: Peter Lang, 2001).

207 *"when it is on me"* Jonathan Swift to Alexander Pope, March 6, 1728–9, in Swift, *Correspondence,* vol. III.

207 *Some doctors prescribed* Wanda J. Creaser, "'The Most Mortifying Malady': Jonathan Swift's Dizzying World and Dublin's Mentally Ill," *Swift Studies: The Annual of the Ehrenpreis Center* 19 (2004). I'm especially grateful to Professor Creaser's article, which is the single best treatment of Swift's illness I've encountered. It was instrumental in confirming several facts in this chapter, and it's a moving description of chronic illness, beautifully written. Other remedies noted in this list were confirmed in Wilde's *Closing Years* and Damrosch's *Jonathan Swift.*

209 *"a hundred oceans"* Jonathan Swift to Henrietta Howard, August 19, 1727, in Swift, *Correspondence,* vol. III.

209 *"Noise of seven Watermills"* Jonathan Swift to Knightley Chetwode, October 1724, in Swift, *Correspondence,* vol. II.

209 *"It is not the deafness"* Robert Weston, *Medical Consulting by Letter in France, 1665–1789* (London: Routledge, 2013).

212 *Jean Pierre Flourens* Robert W. Baloh, *Vertigo: Five Physician Scientists and the Quest for a Cure* (New York: Oxford University Press, 2017).

213   *Prosper Menière lived* Note the variant spelling of his
        name. Somewhere, in subsequent years, the name of the
        disease acquired an acute accent that Menière's own name
        did not possess. I haven't come across commentaries that
        explain it, just commentaries that note it, as I'm doing
        here.

213   *struck by hammers* Lorelle Polano, "Issues in Deafness: An
        Analysis of the Existing Literature Pertaining to Issues
        of the Cultural-Linguistic Definition of Deaf Culture"
        (master's thesis, Toronto Metropolitan University, 2002),
        doi:10.32920/ryerson.14649867.v1.

214   *"indescribable distress"* Baloh, *Vertigo*.

214   *"I walk like a drunken Man"* Jonathan Swift to Rev. Thomas
        Sheridan, September 2, 1727, in Swift, *Correspondence*,
        vol. III.

214   *"had at least half a dozen"* Johnathan Swift to Alexander
        Pope, March 6, 1728–29, in Swift, *Correspondence*, vol. III.

215   *Josef Breuer and Ernst Mach* Baloh, *Vertigo*.

217   *"red plastic material"* Baloh, *Vertigo*.

217   *Anglo-Indian otologist* Baloh, *Vertigo*.

218   *"frustratingly slow"* Carol A. Foster, "Optimal Management
        of Ménière's Sisease," *Therapeutics and Clinical Risk
        Management* 11 (February 25, 2015): 301–07, doi:10.2147/
        TCRM.S59023.

219   *As late as 1994* Baloh, *Vertigo*.

222   *"It would be difficult"* Damrosch, *Jonathan Swift*.

222   *"I have been these five weeks"* Johnathan Swift to Knightley
        Chetwode, January 30, 1721–2, in Swift, *Correspondence*,
        vol. II.

223   *"blindness separates people"* Good luck finding where she
        said it, or *if* she said it, or if she didn't who did.

224   *"a chearfull woman"* Johnathan Swift to Charles Ford,
        October 9, 1733, in Swift, *Correspondence*, vol. III.

224   *"a worthless companion"* Johnathan Swift to Henrietta
        Howard, September 14, 1727, in Swift, *Correspondence*,

vol. III. I understand his reticence well. It's easier to push people away than to wait and see if they'll push you.

224   *"giddiness I was subject"* Johnathan Swift to John Gay and the Duchess of Queensberry, June 29, 1731, in Swift, *Correspondence*, vol. III.

224   *"You healthy People"* Johnathan Swift to Charles Ford, April 4, 1720, in Swift, *Correspondence*, vol. II.

225   *"He talks a great deal"* Creaser, "'Most Mortifying Malady."

225   *Maybe yes and maybe no* Carol A. Foster and Robert E. Breeze, "Endolymphatic Hydrops in Ménière's Disease: Cause, Consequence, or Epiphenomenon?" *Otology & Neurotology* 34, no. 7 (2013): 1210–14, doi:10.1097/MAO.0b013e31829e83df.

225   *"directly responsible"* Saumil N. Merchant et al., "Pathophysiology of Meniere's Syndrome: Are Symptoms Caused by Endolymphatic Hydrops?" *Otology & Neurotology* 26, no. 1 (2005): 74–81, doi:10.1097/00129492-200501000-00013.

226   *"furiously insane"* Wilde, *Closing Years*.

227   *"years and Infirmatyes"* Johnathan Swift to Alexander Pope, December 2, 1736, in *Correspondence of Jonathan Swift, D.D.*, ed. David Woolley, vol. IV (Frankfurt am Main, Germany: Peter Lang, 2007).

227   *"a long Fit of Deafness"* Johnathan Swift to Rev. Thomas Sheridan, April 9, 1737, in Swift, *Correspondence*, vol. IV.

229   *"I will be very Temperate"* Johnathan Swift to Rev. Thomas Sheridan, August 12, 1727), in Swift, *Correspondence*, vol. III.

230   *"I shall be like that tree"* Damrosch, *Jonathan Swift*.

232   *I came across a book* Peggy Rambach, *Fighting Gravity* (Lebanon, NH: Steerforth Press, 2001).

241   *"flighty, scattered thinking"* Louise Hay, *You Too Can Change Your Life* (Carlsbad, CA: Hay House, 1984).

242   *"stating my health issue"* Beatrice T., "I Am Safe: Positive Affirmations to Ease Meniere's Dis-ease," *Menieres: An Inner (Ear) Journey* (blog), June 4, 2012, http://

menieresjourney.blogspot.com/2012/06/i-am-safe-posi-tive-affirmations-to-ease.html.

249   *"where material worlds"* Deborah Kapchan, "Body," in *Keywords in Sound*, ed. David Novak and Matt Sakakeeny (Durham, NC: Duke University Press, 2015).

254   *In the 1830s Georges Cuvier* Although I don't quote directly from the text, to double-check my catastrophic facts I consulted Michael J. Benton, *When Life Nearly Died: The Greatest Mass Extinctiaon of All Time* (London: Thames & Hudson, 2003).

Acknowledgments

The first eyes on everything I write belong to this book's dedicatee, Elisa Gabbert. She has a perfect talent for catching little missteps, hidden contradictions, spelling that is nonstandard, and sentiments that are all too standard. And for keeping my heart in one piece. The book you're holding is dedicated to her for a reason.

Thank you to Noah Ballard for seeing what lay hidden inside the essays I pushed across his desk, and for championing an idiosyncratic story through a tricky period of history, and for always standing up for me. Like an archeologist, Daniel Slager patiently worked at the manuscript with a brush to clear away the sand and excavate the figures underneath. He made this book much better. All his colleagues at Milkweed Editions have been brilliant: Mary Austin Speaker, Broc Rossell, Bailey Hutchinson, Yanna Demkiewicz, Shannon Blackmer, Tijqua Daiker, Katie Hill, and Morgan LaRocca. And thanks to the names there I haven't yet met, but whose bearers help the book meet the world.

Thank you to Mensah Demary for early advocacy at *Catapult*, and to all the editors who published parts of the book before those parts made a whole: Jackson Lears at *Raritan*, Justin Taylor and Minna Proctor at *The Literary Review*, Rachel Riederer, Jennifer Gersten, and Eryn Loeb at *Guernica*, Ron Slate at *On The Seawall*, Essence London and Gionni Ponce at *Indiana Review*. A couple of chapters in the book were so changed from the originals that almost nothing of what was first published now remains; nonetheless, my thanks extend to Stephen Corey and Jenny Gropp at *Georgia Review* and to Kelly Luce and Lincoln Michel at *Electric Literature*.

If I were to have included four more names under Elisa's in the dedication, they'd belong to the co-editors I worked with at the arts journal where I first published the short essay "Losing Music," Steve Donoghue, Rohan Maitzen, Sam Sacks, and Greg Waldmann, who startled me with their encouragement and made me feel as though perhaps I really did have something to say. Thank you also to Lighthouse Writers, my home away from home during my years in Denver, especially to Mike Henry, Andrea Dupree, Genna Kohlhardt, and Torin Jensen. And to the early readers I met via Lighthouse: Michael Catlin, Tim Correll, Jon Leslie, and Dan Manzanares. Tiffany Race and Paulette Harwood and Aaron Angello and Chris Marstall and Melissa Goodrum and Peter McLaughlin and William Dewey and Sara Nassr all read chapters—or in some cases the full manuscript—and offered me their help and reassurance. Socheat

Touch graciously permitted me to quote from her writing. Kevin Caron, Katie Caron, Kirsten Lewis, Gene Baker, Danny Telgarsky, and their partners and families have enriched my whole life—they have my love and they know it. And so do writerly friends Michael Joseph Walsh, Shafer Hall, Adam Golaski, Miriam Suzanne, Chip Cheek and Katie Hunt, Shannon and Tony Mancus, Jeff Eaton and Maureen Thorson, all of whom talked to me about the book and made me feel less alone. Hanif Abdurraqib, M. Leona Godin, Maggie Smith, and Elissa Washuta all generously and thoughtfully endorsed the project—I'll be in their debt for some time, and gladly so.

Teju Cole and Lucas Mann and Mike Meginnis deserve my thanks for their early belief in the book (as does Justin Taylor, who earns his second mention here, but for whom the book may have existed in manuscript alone). For early advice and contacts, thank you also to Rhian Ellis, David Wroblewski, Amanda Rea, and James Scott. Joanna Scott and Rick Koster and Glenn Shea and Cindy Wang Morris offered reassurance when I needed it. Bergin O'Malley walked clear across town to make sure I hadn't left the burner on in James Merrill's apartment, talking me through a nervous drive over the phone. Thank you to Quinton Singer for style points, and thank you to librarians Susan Walker at Yale's Lewis Walpole Library in Farmington and Victoria Rice at the Otis Library in Norwich, Connecticut. Cory Portnuff read the "Sound Shadow" chapter; Dr. Carol Foster and Leo Damrosch read "The Hundred Oceans of Jonathan Swift"; all offered excellent advice; any remaining errors are my own.

Thank you to the residencies that gave me time and space: SPACE in Portland, Maine, the James Merrill House in Stonington, Connecticut, and the Heather Green/Peter Streckfus back porch residency project in Fairfax, Virginia.

Thank you and love to my family: Erin and Brian and Colin and Julianne and Ruby Wise; Mike and Ann Gabbert; and especially to my mother, Linda Cotter, for journeying with me into the cold. And for my first songs.

Last but not least thank you to the wonderful friends with whom I idled afternoons in the early days of the new world. Those names I haven't inscribed above I inscribe below: Adalena Kavanagh, Adam O'Fallon Price, Sebastian Castillo, Brian Hall, Billy Fatzinger, Willie Fitzgerald, David Burr Gerrard, Emily Adrian, Alex Higley, Daniel Hornsby, Isaac Butler, J. Robert Lennon, Lauren Goldenberg, Miranda Popkey, Sandra Newman (and Howard Mittelmark), Steve Himmer, V.V. Ganeshananthan, Michael Schaub, Leela Rice, Tom McAllister, Tracy Rae Bowling, Catherine Nichols. You guys are my lemon and my tangerine.

JOHN COTTER is the author of the novel *Under the Small Lights*. He has contributed essays, theater pieces, and fiction to the *New York Times Magazine, New England Review, Raritan, Guernica, Epoch, Prairie Schooner,* and *Commonweal.* He lives in Providence, Rhode Island.

milkweed
EDITIONS

Founded as a nonprofit organization in 1980,
Milkweed Editions is an independent publisher.
Our mission is to identify, nurture, and publish
transformative literature, and build an engaged
community around it.

Milkweed Editions is based in Bdé Óta Othúŋwe
(Minneapolis) within Mní Sota Makhóčhe, the
traditional homeland of the Dakhóta people. Residing
here since time immemorial, Dakhóta people still
call Mní Sota Makhoče home, with four federally
recognized Dakhóta nations and many more Dakhóta
people residing in what is now the state of Minnesota.
Due to continued legacies of colonization, genocide,
and forced removal, generations of Dakhóta people
remain disenfranchised from their traditional homeland.
Presently, Mní Sota Makhóčhe has become a refuge
and home for many Indigenous nations and peoples,
including seven federally recognized Ojibwe nations.
We humbly encourage our readers to reflect upon the
historical legacies held in the lands they occupy.

milkweed.org

Milkweed Editions, an independent nonprofit literary publisher, gratefully acknowledges sustaining support from our board of directors, the McKnight Foundation, the National Endowment for the Arts, and many generous contributions from foundations, corporations, and thousands of individuals—our readers. This activity is made possible by the voters of Minnesota through a Minnesota State Arts Board Operating Support grant, thanks to a legislative appropriation from the arts and cultural heritage fund.

Interior design and typesetting
by Mary Austin Speaker

Typeset in Adobe Caslon

Adobe Caslon Pro was created by Carol Twombly
for Adobe Systems in 1990. Her design was inspired by
the family of typefaces cut by the celebrated engraver
William Caslon I, whose family foundry served
England with clean, elegant type from the early
Enlightenment through the turn of the
twentieth century.